The company se[cretary's]

desktop guide

Roger Mason

GW00361458

THOROgOOD

First published by Thorogood 1999.
Updated and reprinted 2004

Thorogood, 10-12 Rivington Street
London EC2A 3DU

Telephone: 020 7749 4748
Fax: 020 7729 6110
Email: info@thorogood.ws
Web: www.thorogood.ws

© Roger Mason 2004

All rights reserved. No part of this publication may
be reproduced, stored in a retrieval system or transmitted
in any form or by any means, electronic, photocopying,
recording or otherwise, without the prior permission
of the publisher.

This book is sold subject to the condition that it shall
not, by way of trade or otherwise, be lent, re-sold, hired
out or otherwise circulated without the publisher's prior
consent in any form of binding or cover other than in
which it is published and without a similar condition
including this condition being imposed upon the
subsequent purchaser.

No responsibility for loss occasioned to any person acting
or refraining from action as a result of any material in this
publication can be accepted by the author or publisher.

A CIP catalogue record for this book is
available from the British Library

ISBN 1 85418 284 6

Printed in India by Replika Press Pvt. Ltd.

Designed and typeset by Driftdesign

Special discounts for bulk
quantities of Thorogood books
are available to corporations,
institutions, associations and
other organisations. For more
information contact Thorogood
by telephone on 020 7749 4748,
by fax on 020 7729 6110, or
email us: info@thorogood.ws

About the author

Roger Mason is a highly experienced director and company secretary. His early career was with Midland Bank and the Ford Motor Company before becoming finance director of ITC Entertainment Ltd. He was, for 14 years, company secretary and finance director of a leading British greetings card company. He lectures on finance and business matters and has written a number of books, including the best selling *Credit Controller's Desktop Guide* and *The Complete Guide to Debt Recovery*.

Icons

Throughout the Desktop Guide series of books you will see references and symbols in the margins. These are designed for ease of use and quick reference directing you to key features of the text. The symbols used in this edition are:

 Definition

 Checklist

g Example

Contents

Introduction   1

Important note concerning terms 3

The position of company secretary   5

Introduction 6

Who may hold the position of company secretary? 6

Appointment and removal of the company secretary 7

The company secretary as an officer of the company 8

The statutory duties of the company secretary 8

Other duties of the company secretary 10

Checklist 10

Directors   11

Introduction 12

What makes a person a director? 12

Shadow directors 13

Restrictions and qualifications relating to appointment 14

Appointment of directors 14

Retirement and removal of directors...15

Company secretary's responsibilities on
appointment or removal of a director 17

Rights of directors 17

Responsibilities of directors 19

Miscellaneous matters...20

Checklist 21

3

The statutory registers and the company seal   **23**

Introduction 24

Location, inspection and copies of registers..............................25

Fees permitted for inspection and copies 27

Register of Members 28

Register of Directors and Secretary 29

Register of Directors' Interests....................................31

Register of Interests in Voting Shares 32

Register of Charges 33

Register of Debenture Holders 33

Confidentiality Orders 33

The company seal 34

Checklist 35

4

Accounts   **37**

Introduction 38

Preparing accounts and keeping records 38

Accounting reference date and first accounts 39

Content of accounts 40

The auditor's report..42

Abbreviated accounts and the accounts of small
and medium-sized companies 43

Approval, signature and publication of accounts..........................44

Dormant companies 47

Checklist 48

5

Dividends and interest payments   **51**

Introduction 52

Funds available for payment of dividends and interest 52

The significance of different classes of share 53

Procedure for declaration and payment of dividends...................53

Dividend warrants and tax vouchers 55

Scrip dividends 56

Checklist 56

6

Share capital and shareholders 59

Introduction 60

Authorised share capital 60

Issued share capital 61

Different classes of share 61

Instalments and calls..64

Serious loss of capital by a public company 65

Nominee shareholders...65

The position of minors 66

Checklist 67

7

The issue of shares and the reduction of share capital 69

Introduction 70

Procedures for the issue of shares for cash 70

Procedures for the issue of shares for non-cash consideration.....72

The issue of shares at a premium 73

The issue of shares at a discount 73

Pre-emption rights 74

Financial assistance and the acquisition of a company's shares 75

Reduction of capital..75

Acquisition by a company of its own shares 76

Checklist 77

8

Debentures and loan stock 79

Introduction 80

Definitions and brief descriptions 80

Power to issue debentures...82

Fixed and floating charges 83

Transferability and stamp duty 84

Trustees..84

Trust deed 85

Registration of charges 85

Checklist 86

9

The Memorandum of Association   89

Introduction 90

The name of the company......................................90

Registered office 93

The objects of the company 94

Other clauses in the memorandum 96

Subscription clause...96

Disclosure of information on company stationery 97

Checklist 98

10

Articles of Association   101

Introduction 102

Model sets of articles 102

Freedom to adopt articles 103

Registration procedure and required format of articles 104

Alteration of articles...104

Table A for a company limited by shares 105

Table C for a company limited by guarantee 108

Checklist 109

11

General meetings   111

Introduction 112

The Annual General Meeting 112

An Extraordinary General Meeting 114

Resolutions and notice of resolutions 114

Elective regime 117

Single-member companies.................................119

Convening and requisitioning of meetings.......120

Period of notice and entitlement to receive notice 121

Notice sent by means of electronic communication 123

Details and contents of notice 123

Proxies 124

Quorum 125

Adjournment 126

The chairman... 126

Voting... 127

Minutes 128

Electronic general meetings.. 129

Checklist 130

12 Board meetings

133

Introduction 134

The articles and Table A 134

The calling of Board Meetings and due notice 135

Quorum 136

Directors' interests... 136

The chairman... 137

A deficiency in the number of directors 138

Written resolutions of directors 138

Minutes 138

Committees and other meetings 140

Electronic board meetings 141

Checklist 141

13 Transfer and transmission of shares

143

Introduction 144

Transfer of shares 144

CREST in outline 145

Forged transfers 146

Bearer shares.. 146

Transmission of shares... 147

Share certificates.. 149

Stamp duty 150

Form J30: Stock transfer.. 152

Checklist 154

14

Receivership and administration 155

Introduction 156

Receivership 157

The concept of administration 159

The appointment of an administrator........................159

Grounds for obtaining, and purposes of,
an administration order 160

Effects of administration 161

The early stages of administration 161

The later stages and conclusion of administration 162

Checklist 163

15

Winding up and striking off 165

Introduction 166

Members' voluntary winding up.................................167

Creditors' voluntary winding up.................................168

Winding up by the court 169

The abolition of Crown Preference 170

Order of priority in the distribution of funds 171

Licensed Insolvency Practitioners 172

Striking off following an application by the company 173

Striking off at the instigation of the registrar 174

Checklist 174

16

The annual return 177

Introduction 178

Time limits for filing the annual return.............................178

The shuttle system 179

The annual return in detail 182

Form 363A:Annual return form 186

List of past and present members schedule to form 363A 192

Checklist 193

17

Dealing with Companies House 195

Introduction..196

Companies House forms..197

Requirements to file resolutions.......................................198

Quality of documents filed at Companies House 199

Penalties and prosecutions in connection
with late and non-filing...200

Obtaining information from Companies House 202

Methods of filing..206

Checklist 207

APPENDICES

A

Table A to the Companies Act 1985 209

Regulations for management of a company limited by shares 210

B

Table C to the Companies Act 1985 241

Regulations for management of a company limited
by guarantee and not having a share capital 242

C

Companies House details and guidance booklets 245

Company House addresses 246

Companies House guidance booklets...247

D

**Examples of completed
Companies House forms**   **249**

E

Full list of Companies House forms   **275**

Section A: General forms 276

Section B: Foreign forms 281

Section C: European economic interest grouping forms..........283

Section D: Disqualification forms 284

Section E: Limited partnership forms 284

Section F: Welsh bilingual forms...284

Section G: Investment company with variable
                 capital forms 285

Section H: Limited Liability partnership forms.......................285

Section I: Other forms available 287

F

Company statistics   **289**

Index...293

Introduction

Important note concerning terms

This Guide was first published in 1999 and it has been very successful. Needless to say both Thorogood and I would like to thank everyone who has purchased it, read it and referred to it. The world has moved on and it is now time for an update. In doing this I have brought the detail up-to-date in obvious areas such as addresses and telephone numbers, as well as in such matters as the law concerning a compulsory audit. I have also enlarged the Guide by covering a small number of additional topics, even though the law has not changed. 'Shadow Directors' is an example.

This edition of the Guide includes two extra appendices – the latest Table C and Company Statistics. It has also been updated to reflect (among other things) the following changes made since publication of the first edition:

- The introduction of Confidentiality Orders.

- The abolition of Advance Corporation Tax and the consequences for dividend tax vouchers.

- Implementation of The Companies Act 1985 (Electronic Communications) Order 2000.

- The Enterprise Act 2002 with its effects on liquidation, receivership and administration.

- Changes to the Annual Return and other Companies House forms.

- The development of electronic filing at Companies House.

Most readers will know that a far-reaching examination of company law is very likely to lead to a new Companies Act. This Guide does not anticipate what may (or may not) be in the new Act, but sticks firmly to explaining existing law and good practice. I must, though, mention that it is proposed, foolishly in my opinion, to allow all private companies to operate without a company secretary if they so wish. At least it is *'allow to'* not *'compel to'*.

I realise that nearly all readers will treat this guide rather like a menu. They will not read all of it, or even most of it, but will go straight to a section relevant to a particular problem. This is very sensible and it is why there is a detailed Contents section. The need for this was brought home to me when I put the chapters in order. There did not seem to be strong reasons for placing some chapters ahead of other chapters, although I have put the section on winding up towards the end. It is not like a crime novel where the body is discovered in the first chapter and the butler is revealed as the murderer on the last page.

My first law lecturer told me that, in the context of the law, 'he' meant 'he or she', unless the context indicated otherwise, and that the term male embraced the female. He went on to say that the male embraced the female outside the context of the law as well. In order to avoid numerous qualifications, I have followed this custom and I trust that women company secretaries will understand that no slight is intended. Reference to Table A will show that parliamentary draftsmen (and draftswomen) still follow the practice.

Finally, I would like to thank you for your confidence in selecting this Guide. I hope that you find it very helpful.

Roger Mason

Important note concerning terms

The principal act affecting company law and company secretaries is the Companies Act 1985. In this guide reference to the 'The Act' means The Companies Act 1985 as amended, unless the context indicates otherwise.

chapter one

The position of company secretary

Introduction

Who may hold the position of company secretary?

Appointment and removal of the company secretary

The company secretary as an officer of the company

The statutory duties of the company secretary

Other duties of the company secretary

Checklist

Introduction

Company secretaryship is, like the institution of matrimony, an honourable estate. Not only should every company have one, every company must have one. There are over 1,500,000 companies registered with the Registrar of Companies and all must have a company secretary. If any do not, then an offence has been committed.

The position of company secretary is deeply ingrained into the British system and into the systems of many other countries too. The company secretary's rights, duties and responsibilities are partly fixed by statute and partly by accepted good practice. Although the statutory responsibilities cannot be varied, the remainder can and do vary enormously. This is The Company Secretary's Desktop Guide and it is appropriate to commence with a study of different aspects of this fascinating and unique position.

Who may hold the position of company secretary?

Over 99% of all companies are private companies and almost any person may hold the position of company secretary in them. Of course the directors are always well advised to make a suitable choice and may face criticism if they do not do so.

It is different for public companies, and Section 286 of the Act states that the directors should ensure that the company secretary meets one of the following criteria:

a) held the office of secretary, deputy secretary or assistant secretary of the company on 22 December 1980

b) for at least three of the five years immediately preceding the appointment held the office of secretary of a company other than a private company

c) is a barrister, advocate or solicitor called or admitted in any part of the United Kingdom

d) is a member of one of the following bodies:

   • The Institute of Chartered Accountants in England and Wales

   • The Institute of Chartered Accountants of Scotland

   • The Institute of Chartered Accountants in Ireland

- The Chartered Association of Certified Accountants
- The Institute of Chartered Secretaries and Administrators
- The Institute of Cost and Management Accountants
- The Chartered Institute of Public Finance and Accountancy

e) is a person who, by virtue of his holding or having held any other position or his being a member of any other body, appears to the directors to be capable of discharging those functions.

In respect of all companies, the sole director of a company may not also be company secretary.

A body corporate may be company secretary, so long as the sole director of the body corporate is not also the sole director of the company in question. A partnership may be appointed to the position of company secretary. In England and Wales this has the effect of making all partners joint secretaries, but in Scotland the partnership is appointed in its own right.

Appointment and removal of the company secretary

In the case of a newly formed company, the person named as secretary in the statement accompanying the memorandum and articles for registration becomes, upon registration, the first secretary.

Subsequent appointments, removals, etc are made by a decision of the directors. It is a requirement that these decisions be minuted. The precise procedure may be specified by a company's articles. Table A to the Companies Act 1985 applies unless it is inconsistent with a company's articles. Reg. 99 of Table A states:

> *'Subject to the provisions of the Act, the secretary shall be appointed by the directors for such term, at such remuneration and upon such conditions as they may think fit, and any secretary so appointed may be removed by them.'*

The Registrar of Companies must be notified of an appointment within 14 days and this must be done on form 288a. This form requires the new secretary's signature consenting to the appointment. Resignation or removal of the company secretary must be advised to the Registrar of Companies on form 288b. A change in the secretary's particulars must be advised on form 288c.

The company secretary as an officer of the company

Officers of a company have specially recognised duties and responsibilities, and may incur personal liability and penalties in certain circumstances. This particularly relates to compliance with the provisions of the Companies Act. Directors and the company secretary are always officers of the company, and others may be in some circumstances. Section 744 of the Act defines officer as follows:

> *'in relation to a body corporate, includes a director, manager or secretary'*

The company secretary has statutory responsibilities additional to those given by the Companies Act and the details will vary from company to company. It will depend on employment policies, different industries, etc.

The statutory duties of the company secretary

Overall compliance responsibility lies with the directors and they may, if they wish, do the work themselves. However, it is normal for it to be the responsibility of the company secretary and this is usually the wish of the directors.

The company secretary is generally responsible for keeping the statutory records, sending returns and forms to the Registrar of Companies, generally complying with the Companies Acts, and generally ensuring good (or at least lawful) corporate governance. Beyond this, practice varies and these extra matters are considered in the following section. This section deals with what might be called the statutory duties.

There is no requirement that the company secretary must personally do the necessary work associated with the statutory duties. In some cases the company secretary's signature is required, but not always. Many contracts, legal documents, etc, require the signature of two directors or one director and the secretary. A company secretary who is also a director may not sign such a document in each capacity; a further director's signature is required. In many companies the secretary does personally do the work associated with the statutory duties, but in all cases he should ensure that the work is satisfactorily done.

The following is an outline summary of the secretary's main duties. Each is considered in detail elsewhere in this desktop guide.

- Ensure that the statutory books and registers are kept up to date, in good order and available for inspection.

- Ensure that all necessary forms and other documents for the Registrar of Companies are accurate and submitted on time.

- Ensure safe custody and correct use of the company seal.

- Ensure that the annual return is accurate and submitted on time.

- Attend and take minutes of meetings of members and of the Board. Ensure that such meetings are validly called according to statute and the articles. If necessary, advise the chairman and other directors on correct procedure at such meetings.

- Generally, ensure that the company complies with the provisions of the Companies Act, other legislation and its own memorandum and articles.

- In the case of a public company, ensure compliance with Stock Exchange regulations.

- Ensure that changes in membership are handled correctly and that valid share certificates are issued. Responsibility for this is sometimes passed to a registrar.

- Ensure that dividends are paid correctly and that valid dividend vouchers are issued.

- Ensure that statutory accounts are sent to members in good time and that a signed copy is sent to the Registrar of Companies in good time.

Other duties of the company secretary

Practices vary enormously and in some cases the secretary is responsible for nothing beyond the 'statutory duties.' This is particularly likely to be the case if the secretary is an outsider. In some companies the secretary may be a vital member of the management team with responsibility for one or more of accounts, treasury, property, computers, personnel, training, general administration and other things. The secretary is frequently responsible for matters calling for regulation, compliance and sound administration. Health and safety is one example.

The company secretary may be a director as well as secretary.

Checklist

- Any person may be secretary of a private company.

- This is not the case for a public company where the secretary must be suitably qualified. This is explained in this chapter.

- A sole director may not also be company secretary.

- A company or partnership may be company secretary. Details are in this chapter.

- The first company secretary is named in the statement accompanying the memorandum and articles. Subsequent appointments are made by the directors.

- The Registrar of Companies must be notified of all appointments and changes.

- The company secretary is an officer of the company.

- The company secretary is not required to perform all the statutory duties personally. He is responsible for seeing that they are properly done.

chapter two

Directors

Introduction

What makes a person a director?

Shadow directors

Restrictions and qualifications relating to appointment

Appointment of directors

Retirement and removal of directors

Company secretary's responsibilities on appointment or removal of a director

Rights of directors

Responsibilities of directors

Miscellaneous matters

Checklist

Introduction

A sound working relationship between the company secretary and the directors is important, and particularly important is the relationship between the company secretary and the chairman. In many companies considerable mutual respect has been earned, to the benefit of the company and of all concerned. The fostering of a good relationship is a key part of the company secretary's role and should not be neglected.

It is appropriate that a study of the role of directors forms the second chapter of this guide. Inevitably, this partly consists of the laws and rules governing appointment, removal, rights, conduct, powers and duties, but it also touches on the directors' role and contribution. Compliance duties placed on directors have become, probably with good reason, more onerous, but running the company is their prime purpose. A good company secretary can reduce the burden on directors.

What makes a person a director?

The Act does not define the position of director in detail. In most companies the position is clear and unambiguous: a director is a person properly and formally appointed in accordance with the provisions of the Act and the articles. However, a person may be held to be a director even though these formalities have not been observed. If this is the case he will be a 'de facto director.' Section 741 of the Act states:

> *'In this Act 'director' includes any person occupying the position of director, by whatever name called.'*

This can be extremely important. Directors may in some circumstances be personally liable for the debts of a company, and this can extend to de facto directors.

Some companies give senior employees a title that includes the word 'director,' but do so without actually appointing them to the Board. This may be to impress customers or to increase the status of the people concerned. An example is the title Director of Sales which is not normally a Board appointment. By contrast, Sales Director normally is a Board appointment.

Restrictions and qualifications relating to appointment

Company articles may require directors to conform with certain require-ments. Such restrictions are less common than was formerly the case but may be encountered. An example of such a restriction is a require-ment that a director hold British nationality. Company secretaries should be particularly aware of three possible restrictions:

Undischarged bankrupt

An undischarged bankrupt may not be a director and neither may a person who is the subject of a bankruptcy restriction order. This is a statutory restriction (Company Directors Disqualification Act 1986) and overrides the articles. However, the court can give permission in exceptional cases.

Age restriction

There is no age restriction in a private company unless one is imposed by the articles. No person who has reached the age of 70 may be appointed, or reappointed, to the position of director of a public company, unless approved by the members in a general meeting. Special notice to the members must have been given and this must have stated the age of the prospective director. These restrictions also apply to a private company that is a subsidiary of a public company.

Share qualification

Company articles sometimes require a director to hold a minimum of a specified number of shares in the company. Section 291 of the Act stipulates that such shares must be acquired within two months of the appointment or such lesser period as may be specified by the articles.

Appointment of directors

As explained above, a person may be a director without having been properly appointed. If this happens, he will be a de facto director or a shadow director. Company secretaries should be aware that this is most definitely not good practice. There may be dangers for the company, for the officers of the company and for the de facto director or shadow director. This section does not consider these matters and deals exclu-sively with the correct procedures for appointment. After appointment of the first directors subsequent appointments are in accordance with the provisions of the articles. Table A applies unless it is inconsistent with the articles.

The first directors

The first directors of a company are named in the statement accompanying the memorandum and articles and sent to the Registrar of Companies. This statement is signed by the named directors and constitutes their consent to act.

Appointment by existing directors

It is normal for existing directors to have the power to fill a casual vacancy, or to appoint additional directors up to any maximum number specified by the articles. This power is given by Reg. 79 of Table A. A casual vacancy may be caused by such things as the death, disqualification or removal of an existing director.

Appointment by members

Apart from the filling of casual vacancies by existing directors, new directors are elected by the members. This is normally at an Annual General Meeting, but it may be at an Extraordinary General Meeting. Election is by means of an ordinary resolution, but special notice must be given to the company if the proposal is by a member. The powers of members to appoint a director will, if properly exercised, override the powers of existing directors.

Retirement and removal of directors

The first directors

The first directors retire at the conclusion of the first Annual General Meeting. They may offer themselves for re-election.

Rotation

This is governed by the articles, but it is normal for one third of the directors to retire at the conclusion of each Annual General Meeting. Table A provides for this and also states that all directors retire at the conclusion of the first Annual General Meeting. Retiring directors may offer themselves for re-election.

Removal by the other directors

Company articles sometimes contain a provision that a director may be removed by a vote of the directors. This does not apply unless it is permitted by the articles and it should be noted that Table A does not provide for it.

Removal by the members

Company members may, by ordinary resolution in a general meeting, vote to remove any director. This right overrides any provision in the articles and any agreement with the director. A director facing dismissal in this way has certain rights which are detailed later in this chapter.

Death

This is conclusive and does not need an explanation.

Age

A director ceases to hold office at the conclusion of the Annual General Meeting following the date on which he reaches an age limit stipulated.

Bankruptcy

This normally means the end of an appointment as a director, but in exceptional circumstances a court may allow it to continue.

Disqualification by court order

This may happen for a number of reasons. An example is if a director has been a director of a company that continued to trade whilst insolvent.

Company secretary's responsibilities on appointment or removal of a director

The responsibility of the company secretary in this situation is to take action in three ways:

- The appointment, or resignation or removal, should be properly minuted.

- Details of the change should be entered in the Register of Directors and Secretary.

- The Registrar of Companies should be notified within 14 days of the change. In the case of an appointment this should be done on form 288a which should be signed by the new director to signify his consent to the appointment. In the case of a resignation or removal, notification should be by form 288b. The Registrar of Companies should also be informed (on form 288c) in the case of a change in notifiable details (change of address, for example) of a continuing director.

In the case of a company listed on the London Stock Exchange, the Exchange should be notified by close of business on the following business day.

There are numerous other points that may be considered according to individual circumstances. They include a press release, an announcement to staff, and alteration to bank mandates.

Rights of directors

These include the following:

Access to all information

All directors, including non-executive directors, have full collective responsibility for the running of the company. It follows that all directors have full rights to information. This includes access to the statutory records and to the financial records, but it applies to other information too. Some companies are so big that there may be practical difficulties in achieving this. Nevertheless, all directors have full and equal rights.

Alternate directors

If permitted by the articles, a director may appoint an alternate director to act in his place during his absence. It is sometimes done by directors who spend significant periods abroad or who are otherwise away. The precise procedures depend on the articles.

Remuneration

There is no automatic right for a director to be remunerated for his services as a director. However, such a right may be given by the articles, which may also stipulate whether the amount of such remuneration is to be fixed by the directors or by the members in general meeting. Remuneration for services as a director is a different matter from remuneration as an employee. It is usual for the remuneration of each director to be fixed by the directors as a whole.

Compensation for loss of office

A director may have a right to compensation if he is removed as a director where provision for compensation is made in a service contract. He may also have a right to compensation (both statutory and under the terms of a service contract) if he is dismissed as an employee.

Indemnity and insurance

Section 310 of the Act limits the extent to which a company may indemnify its directors. A limited indemnity is only possible if permitted by the articles. If so permitted, a company may purchase indemnity insurance for the benefit of directors and other company officers. Directors' duties are becoming progressively more onerous and the risks progressively greater. Indemnity insurance is, as a result, becoming of greater importance.

On receipt by the company of a members' resolution to remove a director

The director has the right to receive a copy of the resolution, to have a statement circulated to members and to have a statement read to the meeting or to address the meeting himself. Certain restrictions relating to libel, etc, may in some circumstances modify these rights.

Responsibilities of directors

Directors are required to act within their powers, as laid down by the Companies Acts and by the memorandum and articles of the company. Certain matters are the prerogative of the members in general meeting and company articles may vary these requirements. However, the Act stipulates that certain matters are always the prerogative of members. Directors exceed their authority at their peril.

Directors are required to act in the best interests of the company as a whole. They must not give undue preference to the interests of one section of the members over the interests of other sections. This may cause practical difficulties because directors are sometimes appointed to look after the interests of a major shareholder, employees or some other such section. Nevertheless, they must act in the best interests of the company as a whole.

Directors appoint the company secretary and usually delegate a great deal of authority to him. This particularly relates to their statutory obligations and they should therefore take care to appoint a suitably competent person.

Directors have primary responsibility for the management of the company and for seeing that statutory obligations are fulfilled. The number of statutory obligations are vast and cover for example health and safety, data protection, compliance, etc. They are responsible for good corporate governance, or at the very least lawful corporate governance. An increasing criticism is that the requirements of directors are becoming so numerous and onerous, that they interfere with the general running of the company for the benefit of the members. In most cases, maximising profits is a primary aim and this is the responsibility of the directors.

Miscellaneous matters

Number of directors

A public company must have at least two directors. If the articles permit (which Table A does not), a private company may have just one director and that one director may be the sole member. However, a sole director may not also be company secretary.

Company stationery

It is not a requirement that company stationery show the names of directors. However, if directors' names are shown, the list must be complete, accurate and up to date. In passing, it should be noted that company notepaper must show the exact registered name of the company, the registered number and place of registration, and the address of the registered office.

Loans to directors

In general, loans to directors are prohibited. There are certain exceptions and qualifications to this rule.

Inspection of directors' service contracts

A copy of a director's service contract must be kept at the registered office or at the place where the Register of Members is kept. There are certain exceptions and qualifications to this rule. A director's service contract must be available for inspection by members within normal business hours and without charge.

Checklist

- A good working relationship between the company secretary and the directors (especially the chairman) is very important. Company secretaries should work towards achieving it.

- Despite all their legal responsibilities, directors should not forget their main purpose of actually running the business, usually with a view to maximising profits.

- It is bad practice and dangerous for a company to have a shadow director. Company secretaries should watch for the signs.

- Depending on the articles, directors normally retire every three years, but may offer themselves for re-election.

- There are a number of ways in which directors may resign, retire or become disqualified. Company secretaries should be familiar with them.

- Company secretaries should do certain things on the appointment or removal of a director. The change should be minuted, entered in the Register of Directors and Secretary and the Registrar of Companies notified within 14 days.

- All directors (including non-executive directors) have full responsibilities.

- All directors have full rights of access to accounting records and other information.

- Indemnity insurance for companies' officers is becoming increasingly common and increasingly necessary. It may only be purchased if permitted by the articles.

- A director has rights to make his case to members if the company receives a members' resolution to remove him.

- Directors must always act within their authority as conferred by statute and the memorandum and articles. Company secretaries should be vigilant and offer firm advice if they see a problem.

- Directors must act in the interests of the company as a whole, and not give preference to the interests of one section.

- A public company must have at least two directors. A private company may have just one director, but that person may not also be the company secretary.

chapter three

The statutory registers and the company seal

Introduction

Location, inspection and copies of registers

Fees permitted for inspection and copies

Register of Members

Register of Directors and Secretary

Register of Directors' Interests

Register of Interests in Voting Shares

Register of Charges

Register of Debenture Holders

Confidentiality Orders

The company seal

Checklist

Introduction

The keeping of the statutory registers is a core part of the company secretary's job, and in most cases it is the company secretary who does it. It is important because members, directors, the Government, the Inland Revenue and the world at large are entitled to accurate, up-to-date information. The number and content of the registers is specified by the Act.

Various firms of law stationers produce excellent packs that contain all the registers, correctly headed, together with minute books, blank share certificates, etc. These are recommended for many companies, but may not be adequate for larger companies having many entries to record. Company secretarial software may be more appropriate in these cases, and this is almost universally used in large companies.

The information in the registers is used in compiling the annual return and for various other forms filed with the Registrar of Companies at Companies House. Members and many others have a legitimate use for it; lenders and credit reference agencies being examples. The information may have a commercial value and, for example, the membership lists of the converted building societies have been much in demand.

Company secretaries should take the registers very seriously, because mistakes and out of date information can reflect badly on the company and on themselves. Of course, the flow of information is not entirely within their control: directors and others may not always share their enthusiasm. The company secretary can only enter what he knows, and in some cases he can only enter information that has been notified by the correct person in the correct way. He must not act on reputed information obtained from another source. The company secretary should use his persuasive skills to encourage others to provide all the information promptly. In many cases it may be necessary for him to give directors a list of their obligations and what is required.

The chapter concludes with a study of the company seal and, now that its use is optional, procedures for operating without it. This is almost always in the control of the company secretary and is conveniently studied with the statutory registers.

Location, inspection and copies of registers

The following rules apply:

Register of Members

The register must be kept at the registered office, unless the Registrar of Companies has been informed on form 353 that it is kept elsewhere. A company registered in England and Wales must keep its register in England and Wales. A company registered in Scotland must keep its register in Scotland.

The register may be inspected by both members and non-members. Inspection must be allowed (except when closed as permitted) for a minimum of two hours on each business day.

Copies or extracts may be required by both members and non-members, and these must be provided within ten days.

Register of Directors and Secretary

The register must be kept at the registered office.

The register may be inspected by both members and non-members. Inspection must be allowed for a minimum of two hours on each business day.

There is no obligation on the company to provide copies or extracts. A person inspecting the register may make copies himself.

Register of Directors' Interests

The register must normally be kept at the registered office, but may be kept with the Register of Members if this is kept elsewhere. If the register is not kept at the registered office, the Registrar of Companies must be advised on form 353.

The register may be inspected by both members and non-members. Inspection must be allowed for at least two hours on each business day. The register must be available throughout each Annual General Meeting.

Copies or extracts may be required by both members and non-members, and these must be provided within ten days.

Register of Interests in Voting Shares

The register must be kept at the place where the Register of Directors' Interests is kept.

The register may be inspected by both members and non-members. Inspection must be allowed for a minimum of two hours on each business day.

Copies or extracts may be required by both members and non-members, and these must be provided within ten days.

Register of Charges

The register must be kept at the registered office.

The register may be inspected by both members and non-members. Inspection must be allowed for a minimum of two hours each business day.

There is no obligation for the company to provide copies.

Register of Debenture Holders

The register may be kept at the registered office or elsewhere if the Registrar of Companies has been informed on form 190. A company registered in England and Wales must keep its register in England and Wales. A company registered in Scotland must keep its register in Scotland.

The register may be inspected by any person. Inspection must be allowed (except when closed as permitted) for a minimum of two hours on each business day.

Copies or extracts may be requested by any person. There is no specified time limit in which these must be provided.

Fees permitted for inspection and copies

In practice companies often decide not to make charges. However, they are permitted to charge as follows:

Register of Members

There is no charge to members for inspecting the register. Non-members may be charged £2.50 per hour or per part of an hour.

The permitted charge (to everyone) for copies and extracts is £2.50 for the first 100 entries or part thereof, £20 for the next 1,000 entries or part thereof, and £15 for every further 1,000 entries or part thereof.

Register of Directors and Secretary

There is no charge to members for inspecting the register. Non-members may be charged £2.50 per hour or per part of an hour.

There is no obligation on the company to provide copies, so any charges are a matter of private arrangement.

Register of Directors' Interests

There is no charge to members for inspecting the register. Non-members may be charged £2.50 per hour or per part of an hour.

The permitted charge (to everyone) for copies and extracts is £2.50 for the first 100 entries or part thereof, £20 for the next 1,000 entries or part thereof, and £15 for every further 1,000 entries or part thereof.

Register of Interests in Voting Shares

Any person may inspect the register and there is no charge to any person.

The permitted charge (to everyone) for copies and extracts is £2.50 for the first 100 entries or part thereof, £20 for the next 1,000 entries or part thereof, and £15 for every further 1,000 entries or part thereof.

Register of Charges

There is no charge to members for inspecting the register. Non-members may be charged 5 pence.

There is no obligation on the company to provide copies so any charges are a matter of private arrangement.

Register of Debenture Holders

There is no charge for inspecting the register to members or registered holders of debentures. Others may be charged £2.50 per hour or per part of an hour.

The permitted charge (to everyone) for copies and extracts is £2.50 for the first 100 entries or part thereof, £20 for the next 1,000 entries or part thereof, and £15 for every further 1,000 entries or part thereof.

Register of Members

This is a key register and is compulsory for every company. It must contain:

- *The names and addresses of all members*

  These details are as supplied by the members and it is important that the register be written up exactly in this way. The order of the names, if it is a joint holding, may for example affect voting rights and the rights to receive dividends.

- *The date on which each member was first registered as a member.*

- *The date on which each former member ceased to be a member.*

- *Details of each holding*

  This should specify the class of share, the individual numbers of the shares if applicable, the amount paid up on each share if applicable, and the number of shares held.

The register must contain the above details for each member for a period of 20 years from when he ceased to be a member.

In the now very unusual event of shares having been converted into stock, the amount of stock held by each member must be shown in the register.

If the company becomes a sole-member company, the register must contain a statement to this effect and the date that it occurred. If such a company acquires a second member, the register must contain a statement that it is no longer a sole-member company and the date that the change occurred.

If there are more than 50 members and the names are not kept in alphabetical order, a separate index must be kept.

No notice of any trust should be marked on the register of a company registered in England and Wales. Section 360 is very specific and states 'No notice of any trust, expressed, implied or constructive, shall be entered on the register.' The position is different for companies registered in Scotland, and for these companies notices served on the company must be recorded in the register.

Some companies have a very large number of members, and in such cases as the privatised utility companies it can be a million or more. Such companies, and many smaller companies too, keep their register in a computerised format.

Register of Directors and Secretary

The register must contain the following information in respect of directors, including alternate directors, de facto directors and shadow directors, though in respect of the last two the requirement is likely to be ignored in practice.

1. Present full surname and forenames

2. Any former surname and forenames

It is not necessary to show former names if they have not been used for at least 20 years, or were only used before attainment of the age of 18. Nor is it necessary to show the maiden surname or former married surname of a married woman, or the former name of a peer (if different from his title).

3. Nationality

4. Residential address

The address given should be the real residential address. It should not be a company office unless the person concerned really does reside at company premises. In very limited circumstances a director or company secretary may apply for a Confidentiality Order and details of these are given in a separate section of this chapter.

5. Business occupation

The terms director or company director are often used but this is not correct. It should be the qualification, skill or occupation. For example, the finance director may be described as an accountant. If a person is a director of several companies and has no particular qualification or other occupation, he may be described as 'director of companies'.

6. Other directorships

This must list the exact names of companies of which the director is currently a director, or of which he has been a director within the last 5 years. It is rather like penalty points on a driving licence; they drop off after a period. Directorships of other companies within the same group need not be included. Also, dormant companies need not be included

7. Date of birth

This is always required.

8. Date of appointment

This is unambiguous and is embarrassing in the case of shadow directors, who of course have not been formally appointed.

9. Date of vacation of office

In respect of the secretary it is only necessary to include the present full surname and forenames, any other surname and forenames, and his residential address.

Register of Directors' Interests

The register contains extensive details of all directors' holdings in shares and debentures, and all directors' rights and options to subscribe for shares and debentures. If the company is part of a group, and if the director is a director of both the holding company and a subsidiary company, details must be entered in the register of the holding company, but not necessarily in the register of the subsidiary company. If the company is part of a group, but the director is only a director of the one company, the register of that company must contain details of holdings, rights and options in the shares and debentures of all group companies.

Shares held in the capacity of trustee need not be reported or recorded, provided that the shares are held as a bare trustee or custodian trustee, or as a simple trustee under Scottish law. Holdings, rights and options that must be recorded are those in the name of:

- All directors, including any shadow directors.

- The spouse of any director.

- The infant child of any director.

The law was originally framed at a time when it was reasonable to expect a director to have detailed knowledge of his spouse's financial affairs, and at a time when marital arrangements tended to be less complicated. Some sympathy may be in order for some directors who may not have ready access to the information. Nevertheless, the requirements are in place.

Each director must notify relevant details to the company within five days of appointment. Thereafter he must notify the company of any changes within five days of the date of the change. In both cases Saturdays, Sundays and Bank Holidays are not counted as part of the five days. Notification by the director must be in writing, and the form of the wording must meet certain criteria. The notification must give precise details, including the amount of the consideration.

The company must only amend the register on receipt of a proper notice from a director and not (with certain exceptions) based on knowledge acquired from another source. The company must make the necessary amendments to the register within three days of notification by the director. Some registers can get very complicated and an index must be kept. This must be brought up to date within 14 days.

Register of Interests in Voting Shares

This requirement is only of public companies and the register is sometimes known by different names. The register may have no entries, but it is still a requirement that such a register be kept.

Any person (acting alone or with others) must notify the company when he acquires shares that result in his total holding exceeding three per cent of the total equity. Similarly, any person (acting alone or with others) must notify the company when he disposes of shares and as a result, his total holding falls below three per cent of the equity. A notifiable interest includes shares held by a spouse, an infant child or stepchild, or a person with whom he is acting. This last arrangement is sometimes colloquially known as a 'concert party.'

Notification must be in writing and it must be in a format that meets certain criteria. Notification must be made within two days of the event, and the company must update the register within three days of receipt of the notification. The company may only update the register on receipt of proper notification, not in response to information acquired from another source.

In the case of a public company having a Stock Exchange listing, similar requirements apply when the holding goes above or below ten per cent. In this instance non-beneficial holdings are aggregated with beneficial holdings. A non-beneficial holding is one where the person exercises the rights without being the ultimate beneficiary. A share club manager may be an example of this.

Register of Charges

Every company must maintain a Register of Charges, even if, as is often the case, it contains no entries. Details of each charge entered in the register must contain:

- The amount of the charge. The amount may be limitless as in 'all moneys owed from time to time.'

- A description of the property charged.

- The names of the parties entitled to the charge.

Every company must keep copies of the instruments creating the charges.

Register of Debenture Holders

The keeping of a Register of Debenture holders is not a requirement under the Act, nor are the precise contents stipulated if one is kept. If only one debenture is issued, full details may be entered in the Register of Charges and no separate register is necessary. If, however, several debentures are issued, a separate register is desirable.

Confidentiality Orders

A director, company secretary or representative of an oversea company may apply to the Secretary of State for a Confidentiality Order. Such an application must be on form 723B and be based on a real and justified fear of violence to or harassment of himself or of a person living at his residential address. Confidentiality Orders are not granted lightly and one will be issued only following receipt of a persuasive case and after investigation.

If a Confidentiality Order has been issued, the director, company secretary or representative of an oversea company may supply a service address to the company. This address must be entered in the registers and be made available to the public in this way. It must also be supplied to Companies House and thus made available to the public. The real residential address must be supplied to the company and to Companies House but will not be made available to the public or to members of the company. It will, though, be available to the police and to certain regulatory authorities.

The company seal

The Companies Act 1989 provides that a company need no longer have a company seal. However, a company may continue to have and use a company seal, and many companies do so. If a company seal is used, its design must incorporate the name of the company.

The company seal (when retained) is used on deeds, and also on documents that are not deeds, such as share certificates. The use of the seal is governed by the articles, but it is normal that its use be attested by two directors or by one director and the secretary. However, subject to the articles, this may be delegated. It may be done, for example, when a share certificate is sealed by a registrar.

It is important that accurate and detailed records are kept of the use of the company seal, and this is normally done by the company secretary. If there are not many sealings it is normal for a Board minute to list and approve the sealings since the last Board Meeting. If there are a lot of sealings, it is usual for a separate Seal Register to be kept. Board minutes will then approve blocks of entries in this register. The company seal is important and the company secretary should take care with its use and safe custody.

Companies may operate either without having a company seal, or by having a seal and electing not to use it. A document signed by two directors, or by one director and the secretary, in a form that clearly states that it is executed by the company, will have the same effect as if it had been sealed. A document intended to be a deed, and whose wording makes that fact clear, will upon delivery have the effect of a deed. An example of such wording is:

Executed by ....
Ltd as a deed and signed by:

.... *Director*

.... *Company Secretary*

Records of documents executed without a company seal, but which would have been sealed had a seal been in use, should be kept by the company secretary in the same way as the records of sealings. Similarly, Board approval to such documents should be given in the same way as Board approval is given to sealings. Such documents must be signed by two directors, or by one director and the company secretary. The task cannot be delegated.

Checklist

- The statutory registers are an important part of the company secretary's job. Errors can reflect badly on the company and on him.

- The company secretary partly depends on information that can only be provided by directors and others. He should be persuasive and encourage them to provide it.

- Law stationers provide excellent packs that include the statutory registers. Software is also available.

- The Act stipulates where each register must be kept and when they can be inspected.

- In some cases copies of registers must be provided by companies. Fees may be chargeable.

- The Register of Members is always very important. It provides information for the annual return.

- No notice of any trust may be entered in the Register of Members of a company registered in England and Wales.

- The Register of Directors and Secretary should include details of any shadow director, though in practice this almost never happens

- The Register of Interests in Voting Shares only applies to public companies.

- The custody and control of the company seal (where there is one) is an important responsibility of the company secretary.

- A company seal is not now essential. Company secretaries should be familiar with the requirements if a company does not have a seal, or does not use it.

- Proper records should be kept and approved, whether a seal is used or not.

chapter four

Accounts

Introduction

Preparing accounts and keeping records

Accounting reference date and first accounts

Content of accounts

The auditor's report

Abbreviated accounts and the accounts of small and medium-sized companies

Approval, signature and publication of accounts

Dormant companies

Checklist

Introduction

The role of company secretary is sometimes combined with that of finance director. However, they are two separate functions and this chapter does not assume that the company secretary needs to be familiar with the minutiae of accounting rules and regulations. It is in any case a very big subject. The company secretary does need to be familiar with the outline requirements concerning the content of the accounts, but most especially he needs to be familiar with all the requirements for the timing, approval, filing and distribution of the accounts. This is at the core of the company secretary's job, and of how he is of service to directors who may need to rely on his expertise.

Preparing accounts and keeping records

This is one of the most basic of the responsibilities of company directors. All companies must keep sufficient records to show the following:

- Details, on a day-to-day basis, of all sums received and expended, with information relating to the receipt and expenditure.

- Details of the assets and liabilities of the company and of the financial position of the company.

- Details sufficient to allow accounts to be prepared, consisting of a profit and loss account and balance sheet.

- If the company deals in goods, details of the stock held at the end of the financial year.

- If the company deals in goods, with the exception of retail sales, details of goods sold and purchased.

Company secretaries will realise that these are only the basic requirements. Directors have a duty to manage a company effectively and this will usually involve more than the above. Circumstances vary and what is necessary for one company may not be appropriate for another, but the above are the basic requirements.

Accounting records must be kept for a minimum of three years in the case of a private company, and for a minimum of six years in the case of a public company. These are Companies Act stipulations, but it should be noted that different periods may be dictated by taxation or other requirements.

Accounting records may be kept anywhere that the directors decide and directors must have full and equal access to them. Common sense may in practice slightly modify this requirement, but the principle is clear.

Company directors must, as well as keeping proper accounting records, prepare and present proper accounts. These must be to proper standards as stipulated by the Act, and as described in this chapter.

Accounting reference date and first accounts

Every company must make up its accounts to a date very close to its accounting reference date, the permitted difference being up to seven days either side of it. This seven day leeway enables companies, if they choose, to adjust for factors such as weekends and Bank Holidays.

For newly registered companies, the accounting reference date is automatically the last day of the month in which the anniversary of its incorporation falls. For example, a company registered on January 18 is given the accounting reference date of January 31.

The period covered by the accounts is the accounting reference period and it is the period between two accounting reference dates. A company may, subject to certain restrictions, elect to alter its accounting reference date and thus its accounting reference period. There are no restrictions on a company making changes that shorten its accounting reference period, apart from a requirement that the first accounts cover a period of at least six months from incorporation. Changes that lengthen the accounting reference period may be made subject to the following restrictions:

• The resulting accounting reference period may not be longer than 18 months.

• A change may not be made to a period for which accounts are already overdue.

• The accounting reference period may not be lengthened more than once in a period of five years. There are certain exceptions, the most commonly used one being to permit the alignment of dates of companies within a group.

A company that elects to change its accounting reference date must notify the Registrar of Companies on form 225.

Content of accounts

The Act makes no reference to interim accounts and accounts for internal use only. However, listed companies are subject to certain requirements as to content and timing and good corporate governance is relevant to all companies. This chapter deals exclusively with published accounts.

Accounting standards and the detailed contents of accounts are very big subjects and there is no room in this book for more than an outline. The Act provides that the following must be laid and delivered:

- A profit and loss account, made up to cover the period from the last balance sheet date to a date within seven days of the accounting reference date.

- A balance sheet as at the final date of the profit and loss account period.

- A directors' report.

- An auditor's report.

- A consolidated profit and loss account and balance sheet where required.

Consolidated accounts (group accounts) are required where a company has at least one subsidiary company on the balance sheet date. There are certain exceptions; the most important being that (subject to certain conditions) an intermediary company need not prepare consolidated accounts. It is normally just the top holding company.

There is an overriding requirement that the accounts must give a true and fair view. Any individual failing in the accounts will, if it is sufficiently serious, breach this requirement. The 'true and fair' requirement overrides other considerations.

The directors' report must contain certain information. The following is a very brief summary of the main items that must be included in the directors' report:

- The main activity and any changes in the period.

- A fair review of the business during the year and of the position at the end of the year.

- The names of directors who have held office at any time during the year.

- Details of any important events since the balance sheet date.

- The amount of any recommended dividends.

- Any difference, if in the opinion of the directors, members should be so advised, in the current market value of land compared with its book value. In practice this means if, in the opinion of directors, the difference is material.

- Details of any acquisition of its own shares by the company or its nominees.

- Directors' interests in shares and debentures of the company at the beginning and end of the year if this information is not given elsewhere in the accounts.

- Details of donations for political purposes if they exceed £200.

- Details of donations for charitable purposes within Great Britain if they exceed £200.

- A summary of activities in the field of research and development.

- Details of company policy relating to recruiting, retaining, providing for and training disabled staff. This applies only to companies employing an average of more than 250 within the United Kingdom.

- Details of company actions to provide employees with information relevant to them as employees, consult employees or their representatives, encourage the involvement of employees in the company's performance, and to make employees aware of the financial and economic factors affecting the performance of the company. This applies only to companies employing an average of more than 250 within the United Kingdom.

- An indication of branches outside the United Kingdom. This does not apply to unlimited companies.

- Details of the company's policy on the payment of creditors, and the average number of days' credit outstanding as at the balance sheet date. This applies to public companies, and to subsidiaries of public companies which are not defined as small or medium- sized.

Certain other matters must be disclosed in the accounts. It may be done elsewhere but is usually contained in the notes. Three key points are:

- Details of related undertakings, meaning parent company and subsidiary companies and undertakings in which a minimum interest of 10 per cent is held.

- Details of loans to directors and connected persons.

- Details of directors' emoluments.

The auditor's report

For annual accounts for a period ending after 26 July 2000 (and with certain exceptions), an auditor's report is not required if all the following apply:

- The company is a private company.

- The company is a 'small company' as defined later in this chapter.

- The company had a turnover, in a period of a year, of not more than £1,000,000. (£90,000 for a charity).

A company that complies with the above and which is a charity having gross income in a year between £90,000 and £250,000 is exempt if the directors cause a report to be prepared in accordance with Section 249 and sent to the company's members.

Only persons holding certain approved accountancy qualifications and having a practising certificate may sign an audit report. Such a report, and all copies of it, must state the name of the auditors.

The rights and duties of auditors is too big a subject for detailed comment in this chapter. However, it should be noted that an audit report comments on the accounts and states whether, in the opinion of the auditor, they give a true and fair view. An audit report does not certify the accuracy of the figures, a point which is sometimes not properly appreciated.

Abbreviated accounts and the accounts of small and medium-sized companies

The above section of this chapter sets out the circumstances in which a company may dispense with an auditor's report. This is a separate matter from abbreviated accounts.

Abbreviated accounts are available to small and medium-sized companies, but **not** to:

• A public company.

• A banking company, an insurance company, or a company authorised under the Financial Services Act 1986.

• Companies that are part of a group that includes one of these companies.

The definitions of small and medium-sized companies are:

Small company

A company that satisfies any two of the following three conditions, for both the current financial year and the previous financial year:

• Turnover not more than £2,800,000.

• Balance sheet total not more than £1,400,000.

• Average number of employees not more than 50.

Medium-sized company

A company that satisfies any two of the following three conditions, for both the current financial year and the previous financial year:

• Turnover not more than £11,200,000.

• Balance sheet total not more than £5,600,000.

• Average number of employees not more than 250.

The privilege of abbreviated accounts relates to accounts sent to the Registrar of Companies, and thus placed on public record. It does not apply to the accounts sent to company members. There is therefore no saving of work and the only benefit is privacy. A company need not take advantage of any or all of the privileges of abbreviated accounts. In summary, these are:

Small company

- No profit and loss account is necessary.

- No directors' report is necessary.

- The balance sheet and notes may be in summarised form.

Medium-sized company

Certain information relating to the profit and loss account need not be disclosed. In particular, it is not necessary to show turnover, other operating income and cost of sales. The balance sheet notes must be shown in full.

The auditor's report accompanying abbreviated accounts must state that, in the opinion of the auditor, the company is entitled to file abbreviated accounts and that the accounts are properly prepared. The accounts must prominently state that they are in accordance with special provisions relating to small or medium-sized companies.

Approval, signature and publication of accounts

Both the balance sheet and the directors' report must be formally approved by the Board of Directors. In practice, approval of the balance sheet signifies approval of the whole accounts. The approvals must be minuted.

The balance sheet should be signed by one director on behalf of the Board. The directors' report should be signed by one director or by the company secretary on behalf of the Board. The copy of the accounts sent to the Registrar of Companies must have signatures and the signature of the auditor. All other copies may carry the printed names rather than signatures. In practice it is usual to have three sets of accounts containing signatures; one each for the Registrar of Companies, the auditor, and for retention by the company itself.

Publication of the accounts is to the members, and to the world at large via the medium of the Registrar of Companies. They are two different processes and will be considered separately.

Filing of accounts with the Registrar of Companies

A private company must file accounts with the Registrar of Companies within ten months of the end of its accounting reference period. A public company must do so within seven months of the end of its accounting reference period. In both cases the directors may claim a three month extension if the company had exports or overseas interests. The directors may claim the extension by submitting form 244 to Companies House. This only has effect for one year and must be delivered before submission is overdue.

Civil penalties are progressively levied on the company if the accounts are delivered late. In addition the directors are liable to criminal charges, though in practice prosecutions are rare. It should be noted that accounts must be received by the due date. Merely posting the accounts by the due date is not sufficient. If the accounts are posted, it is good practice to request a receipt and to make enquiries if it does not arrive.

The seven and ten month periods are calculated from the numerical date, not from the last date of the month. This means, for example, that if the end of the reference period is February 28, accounts must be filed by September 28 or December 28. Accounts filed on September 29 or December 29 are deemed to be late and penalties are levied. Many companies are caught out by this. In certain very tightly defined circumstances Companies House may waive the penalty.

The amounts of the civil penalties depend on the period that submission is overdue. They are as follows:

Length of period	Public company	Private company
Not more than 3 months	£500	£100
Between 3 and 6 months	£1,000	£250
Between 6 and 12 months	£2,000	£500
More than 12 months	£5,000	£1,000

There are special time limits for filing the accounts of newly incorporated companies. If the first accounts cover a period longer than 12 months, accounts must be filed by whichever is the later of:

- Ten months from the first anniversary of incorporation (seven months for a public company).

- Three months from the end of the first accounting reference period.

It is the job of the Registrar of Companies to file the accounts, not to check the accounts. If the accounts contain a mistake, there is a high chance that they will be filed as submitted. If a mistake is very obvious, such as the accounts being seriously incomplete, the Registrar may reject them or raise a query.

Publication of accounts to members

The time limits for doing this are the same as the time limits for sending the accounts to the Registrar of Companies; namely:

- A private company must do so within ten months of the end of the accounting reference period.

- A public company must do so within seven months of the end of the accounting reference period.

In both cases an extra three months may be taken if the company has exports or overseas interests and form 244 has been delivered to the Registrar of Companies. The time limit for a listed public company is six months, but this is a Stock Exchange requirement, not a Companies Act requirement.

Publication of the accounts is the responsibility of the directors. So long as both are done within the permitted time limit, the accounts may be sent to the Registrar of Companies before, after or at the same time as they are laid before the members.

A copy of the accounts must be sent to every member and debenture holder, and this must be done at least 21 days before the meeting at which they are to be laid. Over and above this obligation, any member or debenture holder may at any time request a copy of the latest accounts. The company is obliged to provide such a copy within seven days of receipt of the request.

It is normal to lay the accounts at the Annual General Meeting, but it does not necessarily have to be the Annual General Meeting. Any properly constituted general meeting will suffice.

It is normal practice for a resolution at the general meeting to either accept the accounts, receive the accounts or adopt the accounts. However, such a resolution has little if any practical effect. The accounts are the responsibility of the directors. They have been signed prior to the meeting, and may have been sent to the Registrar of Companies prior to the meeting. The rejection of such a motion is a snub to the directors but has little other effect. The directors have fulfilled their obligations by laying the accounts. Of course, the passing of such a resolution makes clear that the members are voting to accept that the accounts have been formally and correctly laid, and it is therefore good practice. Directors are still responsible for errors in the content of the accounts, even if they have been correctly laid and accepted.

Dormant companies

Subject to certain conditions the accounts of a dormant company need not be audited. The conditions are:

- It must qualify as a 'small company', as defined elsewhere in this chapter, for the accounts period in which it became dormant.

- It has been dormant since the end of that accounts period.

- It was not required to prepare group accounts for the period.

- It is not a banking or insurance company, and it is not authorised under the Financial Services Act.

- It has not made any significant accounting transactions at all in the period.

It is still a requirement that unaudited accounts be filed with the Registrar of Companies and laid before the members in a general meeting. Such accounts must include a prominent statement that the company was dormant throughout the period.

Checklist

- The timing, approval, signature, filing and distribution of accounts are important responsibilities of the company secretary. Directors may need to rely on his expertise.

- All companies are required to keep sufficient basic accounting records.

- Companies are required to prepare and present proper accounts.

- Each company must make up accounts for an accounting reference period terminating on a specified accounting reference date. Seven days leeway either way is permitted.

- Companies may, subject to restrictions and safeguards, change the accounting reference date.

- There is an overriding requirement that accounts must give a 'true and fair view'. A report on this is the primary responsibility of the auditor.

- The Act specifies the minimum content of the accounts and certain things that must be in the directors' report.

- An auditor's report is necessary unless it is a private company and turnover is less than £1,000,000. Other conditions apply.

- 'Small companies' and 'medium-sized companies' may send abbreviated accounts to the Registrar, but not to the members.

- The balance sheet and the directors' report should be approved by the Board and signed on behalf of the Board.

- Accounts with signatures should be sent to the Registrar, kept by the auditor and kept by the company itself. Other copies of the accounts may have printed names.

- A private company must file accounts with the Registrar within ten months of the accounting reference date. For a public company it is seven months.

- An extension of three months is permitted if the company has exports or overseas interests and form 244 has been made to the Registrar of Companies.

- The same limits apply for sending accounts to the members, but this can be done at a time different from the time that they are sent to the Registrar.

- It is the job of the Registrar to file the accounts, not to check them.

- Accounts must be sent to every member and debenture holder, and this must be done at least 21 days before the general meeting at which they are to be laid.

chapter five

Dividends and interest payments

Introduction

Funds available for payment of
dividends and interest

The significance of different classes of share

Procedure for declaration and payment of dividends

Dividend warrants and tax vouchers

Scrip dividends

Checklist

Introduction

This chapter is only relevant to companies having a share capital. It is not relevant to companies limited by guarantee which, of course, do not pay dividends.

It is the signature of the company secretary that is normally printed on the dividend warrant and the company secretary will be heavily involved in administering the payment of dividends. It is important that dividends are paid in accordance with the provisions of the articles and the company secretary may be required to advise on this and on important legal points. He may also need to ensure that the company fulfils its obligations to the Inland Revenue.

Funds available for payment of dividends and interest

Dividends must not be paid out of capital. They may only be paid out of net distributable realised profits, either made in the current year or retained from previous years. It is an important distinction which directors must observe. Company secretaries may sometimes need to advise on the point. Section 263 of the Act states:

> *'a company's profits available for distribution are its accumulated, realised profits, so far as not previously utilised by distribution or capitalisation, less its accumulated, realised losses, so far as not previously written off in a reduction or reorganisation of capital duly made.'*

Precise interpretation of accumulated, realised profits can be very technical, but this is the legal requirement. Section 264 of the Act gives a further and slightly more restrictive requirement for public companies. Such companies may only pay a dividend provided that it does not result in their net assets being less than the aggregate of called-up share capital and undistributable reserves.

Payment of interest on loan stock and debentures is not restricted by the requirement to pay only out of retained, distributable profits. Such payments discharge debts of the company and are not a distribution of profits.

The significance of different classes of share

Many company secretaries will have played the game 'Monopoly' as children or perhaps as adults. They may, like the writer, have drawn the Community Chest card that states 'Receive Interest on seven per cent Preference Shares £25' and, also like the writer, first realised that not all types of share are the same.

If there is only one class of share, problems do not arise, but if there is more than one class of share, directors must pay close attention to the articles. Some types of share receive dividends of a fixed amount or fixed percentage, and some types of share rank before other types of share. There may be more than one type of preference share and they may not, or may, rank equally between themselves. The term 'preference share' implies that this type of share receives a dividend before any remaining profits are available to pay a dividend on ordinary shares. It is possible that a company may have several classes of share. Directors, advised by the company secretary if necessary, must pay close attention to the articles when paying dividends.

Preference shares may be cumulative or non-cumulative. If they are non-cumulative and if a dividend is missed due to a shortage of retained, distributable profits, then the dividend is permanently lost. But if the preference shares are cumulative, a missed dividend must be made up out of distributable profits made in the future. This obligation ranks before the payment of dividends on ordinary shares.

Preference shares are deemed to be cumulative unless the articles make it clear that this is not the case. So the Monopoly player with the Community Chest card may get his £25, even if it cannot be paid at once.

Procedure for declaration and payment of dividends

Declaration and payment of dividends must be done according to the provisions of the articles. The requirements of Table A are, in practice, followed by the articles of many companies.

Table A provides that an interim dividend may be declared and paid by the directors. A final dividend must be recommended by the directors, but this is subject to the approval of members in a general meeting. The members may reject the proposed dividend or reduce the amount of a dividend recommended by the directors, but they may not increase it. In the case of an impasse, the only remedy available to the members is to replace the directors with persons willing to recommend a higher amount.

The date for payment of the dividend is fixed at the time that the dividend is declared. Also fixed at the same time is the date at which names on the share register qualify to receive the dividend. This is obviously important as the sale of shares just before or just after the date may determine whether the buyer or the seller receives the dividend. In practice the parties in the purchase and sale of shares in a private company often fix the matter between themselves. In the case of a public company quoted on a Stock Exchange, it is done according to formal rules.

Resolutions concerning the payment of dividends must be properly minuted. Examples of such directors' minutes are:

> *'It was resolved that an interim dividend in respect of the year ended .... on the ordinary share capital of the company, at the rate of 60 pence per share, be declared payable on .... to shareholders registered at the close of business on ....'.*

> *'It was resolved that a final dividend in respect of the year ended .... on the ordinary share capital of the company, at the rate of 40 pence per share, be recommended to the members at the Annual General Meeting to be held on .... This recommended dividend is to be paid on .... to members registered at close of business on ....'*

In the case of a company having few shareholders it is normal to make the payments by cheque. In other cases it is normal to do so, where possible, by means of bank transfers. Tax vouchers are always required and these are covered in the next section of this chapter.

Dividend warrants and tax vouchers

The traditional method of payment of a dividend is by means of a cheque, known as a dividend warrant. Many companies still do make payments in this way, but the alternative of a direct bank transfer, in accordance with instructions given in a mandate by the shareholder, is becoming more and more common.

It is a legal requirement that warrants issued in connection with the payment of a dividend must be accompanied by a document usually described as a tax voucher. Such a document must be sent to shareholders when the payments are made by means of bank transfers. A tax voucher must also be sent if the payment is of interest rather than of a dividend. It is now possible to send tax vouchers on an annual basis rather than accompanying each payment.

A tax voucher is a statement addressed to the shareholder (or stock-holder) setting out the number of shares (or amount of stock) on which the payment is calculated. It must state the tax credit (if the payment is a dividend), or the tax deducted (if the payment is interest) and the net amount payable.

In the case of interest payments, the gross amount payable is also shown and the tax voucher includes a certificate to the effect that the tax deducted will be accounted for to the Inland Revenue.

Advance Corporation Tax was abolished with effect from April 1999 and a tax voucher in respect of a dividend payment now refers to a tax credit. According to the tax law and rates at the time, the shareholder may have to pay higher rate tax on the dividend or may be entitled to recover some or all of the tax. He will in any case need to retain the voucher as evidence.

Shareholders may, from time to time, lose tax vouchers and request duplicates. A company may issue a duplicate so long as it is marked that it is a duplicate voucher. No indemnity is necessary.

Scrip dividends

A scrip dividend is an issue of further shares rather than a cash distribution. Scrip dividends are sometimes attractive to companies because cash is retained in the company. Tax is payable on scrip dividends, but they are a cost-effective way of reinvesting dividends in the company. For this reason they are attractive to some shareholders.

A scrip dividend is a bonus issue of shares. The company must have sufficient authorised but unissued share capital, and such an issue must be permitted by the articles. Sanction by the members in general meeting is normally required.

Sometimes members are given the choice of taking a dividend in this way, rather than in cash. Furthermore, members may be permitted to give the company a standing instruction that all dividends will be taken in this way until the instruction is changed.

Checklist

• The company secretary has an important role. He may need to advise directors and is normally responsible for administering dividend payments.

• Dividends must not be paid out of capital – but this does not apply to interest.

• Dividends may only be paid out of retained, distributable profits.

• Close attention must be paid to the rights of different classes of share. Preference dividends are normally (but not always) cumulative and rank before dividends on ordinary shares.

• Many companies follow Table A. This permits interim dividends to be declared and paid by the directors.

• Table A requires directors to recommend the amount of a final dividend. Members in a general meeting may reduce the amount, but not increase it.

• Resolutions relating to dividends should be properly minuted.

- A tax voucher must be sent to every shareholder – even if payments have been sent to bank accounts.

- Tax vouchers must give full details – including details of the tax credit.

- Shareholders may sometimes take bonus shares instead of cash. This is known as a scrip dividend.

chapter six

Share capital and shareholders

Introduction

Authorised share capital

Issued share capital

Different classes of share

Instalments and calls

Serious loss of capital by a public company

Nominee shareholders

The position of minors

Checklist

Introduction

The terms 'member' and 'shareholder' are sometimes treated as being interchangeable. This is not always correct because a company limited by guarantee does not have shares or shareholders and, of course, it does not pay dividends. This chapter relates exclusively to companies having a share capital. Such companies account for 96% of all companies incorporated in Great Britain.

A company's share capital and its shareholders are of great importance to the company secretary. They are at the heart of his responsibilities and there are many pitfalls of which he should be aware. The company secretary should be in a position to offer sound advice, and to take the lead in ensuring that the company complies with the letter of the law and with the letter of its articles. He will fulfil a particularly valuable function if, additionally, he can anticipate queries and problems before they become an issue.

Authorised share capital

A company's memorandum must, if it is a company having a share capital, state the total amount of the authorised share capital and how it is divided into shares of a fixed amount. This may, for example, be expressed as '*£1,000,000 divided into 2,000,000 shares of 50 pence each*'. Authorised capital is also known as nominal capital.

The authorised share capital may later be increased if this is permitted by the articles. Reg.32 of Table A does permit the share capital to be increased. Section 121 of the Act states that an increase in the authorised share capital must be exercised by the company in general meeting. This is done by means of an ordinary resolution. The Registrar of Companies must be informed by means of form 123 and provided with a copy of the resolution within 15 days of it being passed. He must also be advised of the classes of shares concerned and any conditions relating to the issue of any new shares.

As the word 'authorised' implies, it is not permitted to issue shares in excess of the authorised share capital. However, it is normally relatively simple to increase the amount of the authorised share capital. It is common for the memorandum to fix the authorised share capital at an amount higher than initially required. This is done so that further shares may easily be issued later if required.

Issued share capital

This is the part of the authorised share capital that has actually been issued. It may be 100 per cent of the authorised share capital, but not more than this. The issued share capital may be divided into different classes of share. The annual accounts and certain other documents, must give full details, broken down by class of share, of authorised and issued share capital.

Different classes of share

It is important to note that the title of a share may be misleading, although in most cases it is not. Nevertheless, a share called a 'preference share' may not have preferential rights at all, or it may have preferential rights in some respects, but not in other respects. The source of the rights, privileges and obligations of a particular class of share may be derived from one of the following:

- The memorandum (although in practice this is rare)

- The articles (this is usual)

- The resolution of members that created additional shares.

The rights of each class of share are interpreted strictly. Unless a right is specifically given, it will almost certainly not be implied. For example, a preferential right to receive a dividend will not normally be taken as implying a preferential right to return of capital in the event of a winding-up. However, preference shares normally have a cumulative right to a dividend unless the contrary is stated. This means that a missed dividend is made up before dividends are paid on other classes of share. Different classes of share will rank equally unless specific rights are given.

It is important that the memorandum, articles or resolution be carefully drafted to achieve exactly the desired rights and obligations; no more and no less. Company secretaries may need to advise on this. There are a number of matters where the rights of the different classes of share may differ, but the following are particularly important:

- Rights to share in a distribution of profits.

- Rights to return of capital in the event of the company being wound up.

- Rights to attend meetings, vote at meetings and participate in the governance of the company.

The following are the principal types of share that may be encountered:

Preference shares

These normally have a right to receive a dividend (either a fixed percentage or calculated in a specified way) that ranks before the rights of ordinary shares. There may be more than one class of preference share, with the rights of one ranking before the rights of another.

The rights to receive a dividend may be cumulative, which means that a missed dividend is made up later if distributable profits become available. If the shares are non-cumulative, a missed dividend is permanently lost.

Preference shares frequently, but not always, carry preferential rights to the return of capital in the event of the company being wound up. Such rights rank behind those of creditors, but ahead of those of ordinary shares.

Preference shares are sometimes convertible to ordinary shares if specified events occur. This could be, for example, the floating of the company on a Stock Exchange. So long as conversion does not take place they continue to receive preferential dividends, but do not have the rights attaching to ordinary shares.

Preference shares may or may not be redeemable. Redemption may be at a fixed point in time, at the option of the company or in certain specified circumstances. Redemption takes place by the return of the capital and the cancellation of the shares. This can be very significant if economic circumstances change. Shares issued with a high rate of interest (known as a high coupon) can be expensive to a company (and hence to the ordinary shareholders) when interest rates are low and in times of low inflation.

The holders of preference shares normally have rights to receive copies of accounts and other specified rights. However, they do not normally have rights to attend meetings or to vote at meetings, except on certain specified matters that directly affect them. This includes changes that affect their shares. Rights to vote at meetings are often given if a preference dividend has not been paid a certain number of days after it became payable.

Ordinary shares

If there is only one class of share, then the shares are ordinary shares. They may be described simply as 'shares' as there is no need to differentiate them from other shares.

Ordinary shares rank behind preference shares in the right to receive dividends. They are highly geared compared with preference shares. If distributable profits are £600,000 and the preference shares have rights to a dividend of £500,000, the ordinary shares 'own' £100,000. If distributable profits rise to £2,000,000 the preference shares will still receive a dividend of £500,000. The same ordinary shares will then 'own' £1,500,000.

Ordinary shares rank behind creditors, and normally behind preference shares, in the event of the company being wound up. If there is insufficient money to pay the ordinary shareholders in full, they suffer the shortage. If there is a surplus they share it between them.

The holders of ordinary shares normally have full rights as to attendance and voting at meetings, and in the general governance of the company. These rights may be diluted if a preference dividend is missed, or some other event occurs that enables the holders of preference shares to acquire voting rights.

Non-voting shares

Voting rights may be restricted or they may be non-existent. Such shares may acquire voting rights if specified events happen. Such shares otherwise normally have the same rights as the other ordinary shares, but they do not carry the same rights to vote in general meetings.

Shares with restricted voting rights are not so common as was formerly the case, and are discouraged by Stock Exchanges. Some such shares have been in existence for a long time, and in some cases steps are taken to give them votes. The long-running campaign to enfranchise the Savoy shares was an example of what can happen.

Shares carrying multiple votes

This is the obverse of non-voting shares. Such shares normally otherwise carry the same rights as other ordinary shares, but have a disproportionate number of votes.

Instalments and calls

Instalments or calls occur when payment in full is not required upon application or acceptance.

Shares may be issued on the basis that payments of specified amounts are due on specified dates. Certain privatisation issues were structured in this way because the Government wanted to increase the attractions of the issues. The precise rules relating to instalments will depend on the articles and in many instances companies follow Table A. They also, of course, depend on the terms of issue. Under Table A, shares may be forfeited if instalments are not paid, and interest may be payable if instalments are paid late. Also under Table A, votes may not be cast in respect of shares with instalments outstanding.

The issue of partly paid shares is now less common than was formerly the case. When it does happen, the directors may 'call' the balance of the shares when they consider it necessary or desirable to do so. Such calls may be for the balance outstanding to be paid completely or for it to be paid in instalments. A call may be for only part of the balance outstanding to be paid, leaving the remainder uncalled.

The procedures for calls are governed by the articles, and in many cases companies follow Table A. This requires at least 14 days notice of a call to be given, and provides for interest to be payable in the event of late payment. It also provides for joint holders to be jointly and severally liable for calls, and for the forfeiture of shares in the event of non-payment. Reg. 8 of Table A provides for the company to have a first and paramount lien on every share (not being a fully paid share), for all moneys (whether presently payable or not) payable at a fixed time or called in respect of that share.

Serious loss of capital by a public company

Directors of a public company are required to call a general meeting if they have reason to believe that the company's net assets have fallen to a figure that is less than half of its called up share capital. This must be done within 28 days of any director becoming aware of the fact, and the meeting must be called for a date within 56 days of any director becoming aware of the fact.

At the meeting the members may consider the situation and decide what, if any, steps they wish to be taken.

This requirement applies only to public companies.

Nominee shareholders

It is fairly common for the beneficial owner of shares to appoint a nominee to hold the shares for him. There are many possible reasons for this. One may be a wish for secrecy or privacy. Another may be administrative convenience. It is extremely common, and perhaps even required, for shares held by stockbrokers, investment managers, in personal equity plans, etc. There has been some unease that requirements for beneficial owners to use nominees increases the isolation of shareholders from companies, and creates problems with such matters as voting and the flow of information.

English companies are not allowed to enter any notice of trust on to the Register of Members, even if they have been notified of the information. The position is different under Scottish law where such notice may be entered on the register if the articles permit. A company should deal exclusively with the body or person named in its register, even if the word 'nominee' appears in its name, and even if the company knows, or believes, that it is acting in the capacity of a nominee.

Notwithstanding the above, directors are required to notify the company of beneficial holdings in the shares of the company. Persons having a beneficial interest of 3 per cent or more in a public company are required to notify the company. Both these matters must be recorded by the company in the appropriate registers. Fuller details are given in Chapter 3.

The position of minors

As readers will know, a minor is a person who has not attained full legal status because of his age. At present this occurs on a person's eighteenth birthday. After that age a person is fully responsible for contracts that they make.

A minor may be a member of a company, but he may repudiate membership and the obligations of membership at any time before his eighteenth birthday or very soon afterwards. Such obligations may include the requirement to pay a call on his shares. If he has not repudiated membership by his eighteenth birthday or soon afterwards, he will assume the full obligations of his ownership.

Although a minor may be a member of a company, there is no obligation on a company to accept a minor as a member. In practice most companies do not accept a minor as a member, although there are no problems with a nominee holding and a minor as the beneficial owner.

It sometimes happens that a minor becomes a member without a company being aware of the fact. In these circumstances the company may act if and when the true position becomes known, and it may do so at any time before the minor reaches his eighteenth birthday. The company may remove the minor's name from the register of members, and restore the name of the person from whom he acquired the shares.

If a company registers a minor as a member whilst knowing that he is a minor, it cannot afterwards repudiate the decision. A minor who is properly registered as a member may exercise rights of membership, including receipt of dividends. Subject to any restrictions in the articles, a minor may vote at meetings. A company should not accept a transfer of shares purported to be made by a person known to be a minor.

Checklist

- Issued share capital must not be greater than authorised share capital.

- It is usually not difficult to increase the authorised share capital.

- Company secretaries should be familiar with the different types of share.

- Titles of shares may be misleading. Rights are strictly interpreted and depend on the memorandum, the articles or the resolution that created them.

- Preference shares normally have preferential rights to receive dividends. Often (but not always) they have preferential rights to the return of capital.

- Preference share dividends are cumulative, unless the contrary is specified.

- Ordinary shares normally have the main voting rights.

- Non-voting shares (other than preference shares) are rare.

- Calls are now relatively rare.

- Under Table A, shares may be forfeited if calls or instalments are not paid. Also, interest may be payable.

- Under Table A, votes may not be cast if calls or instalments are not paid.

- Directors (and the company secretary) of a public company must act immediately if net assets fall to half of called-up share capital.

- Nominees are common and cause few problems. An English company must not enter a notice of trust on to its Register of Members.

- Minors may be shareholders, but companies are not compelled to register them.

The word 'director' in a person's title does not automatically make that person a director in the legal sense. Care should always be taken as it may sometimes have unintended consequences. An outsider may be led into believing that the person concerned is a director in the legal sense and may justifiably believe that he has authority to commit the company. It depends on individual circumstances.

Shadow directors

Section 741 of the Act defines a shadow director as follows:

'In relation to a company 'shadow director' means a person in accordance with whose directions or instructions the directors of the company are accustomed to act'.

An example of a shadow director may be a majority shareholder who is not a properly appointed director, but who gives repeated instructions to the directors which they accept and follow. He would not be a shadow director if the directors did not follow his instructions.

It is bad practice and dangerous for a company to have a shadow director, bad for the company, bad for the directors and bad for the shadow director himself. A shadow director runs particular risks, including the risk of being personally liable for the debts if there is improper activity resulting in the company becoming insolvent.

chapter seven

The issue of shares and the reduction of share capital

Introduction

Procedures for the issue of shares for cash

Procedures for the issue of shares for
non-cash consideration

The issue of shares at a premium

The issue of shares at a discount

Pre-emption rights

Financial assistance and the acquisition of
a company's shares

Reduction of capital

Acquisition by a company of its own shares

Checklist

Introduction

This chapter looks at two specific aspects of share capital; namely its issue and reduction. The company secretary is bound to be closely involved at each step of either process. They are rather technical subjects and it is important that the Act and relevant articles are followed closely. There may be significant penalties for mistakes.

Procedures for the issue of shares for cash

Directors should check the following points and proceed as indicated:

- The issue must not result in the issued share capital being greater than the authorised share capital. If this would be the result, the authorised share capital may be increased as described in the previous chapter.

- The issue of shares must be in accordance with the authority given by the articles, or by an ordinary resolution of the members in a general meeting. This applies to the principle of issue and also to the details of issue.

- Authority may be conditional or unconditional. It must specify the maximum number of shares to be issued and the date that the authority expires. The authority may not last for longer than five years unless it is in accordance with the elective provisions of Section 80A. The authority may be cancelled, varied or extended by a further ordinary resolution of the members.

- A private company may not offer its shares to the public.

- A person applying for shares should be required to complete a suitable application form and submit it to the company with payment for the required amount. If the shares are to be issued fully paid, payment in full is required. If the shares are to be issued partly paid, only part payment is required.

- The directors should pass a resolution that allots the shares and authorises the issue of the share certificates. Applications may be withdrawn until applicants have been notified that this has been done.

- Directors have no authority to allot shares unless this has been given by the articles or by an ordinary resolution of the members in a general meeting. This is with the exception of subscribers' shares and shares allotted in accordance with an employees' share scheme.

- The grant of a right to subscribe for shares, or an option to subscribe for shares, is equivalent to the allotment of shares. It must be authorised in the same way.

- Successful applicants should be informed that their applications have been accepted, share certificates should be issued and the Register of Members should be written up accordingly.

- Unsuccessful applicants should be notified and their payments should be returned.

- Form 88(2), which relates to return of allotments, must be filed with the Registrar of Companies within one month of the allotment. If the total shares have not been allotted within one month, form 88(2) must be returned, showing details of shares that have been allotted. This must be done every month until allotment is complete.

The above relates to both private and public companies. The following additional requirements relate to public companies only:

- Shares may not be allotted unless subscription has been made for the minimum amount specified by the prospectus.

- Shares may not be allotted unless payment has actually been received by the company.

Directors normally have authority to decide the basis on which shares are to be allotted. They may, for example, wish to have a large number of shareholders in order to promote recognition of company products. On the other hand, they may want a small number of shareholders in order to keep costs down.

It is not permitted to offer shares at a discount. It is permitted to offer shares at a premium and this is covered in a separate section of this chapter. Pre-emption rights are also covered in a separate section of this chapter.

Procedures for the issue of shares for non-cash consideration

The issue of shares for non-cash consideration is common in agreed or hostile take-overs. It may be partly for shares and partly for cash, or sometimes all for shares. Sometimes shareholders in the company concerned are given a cash or shares option. Another type of issue of shares for non-cash consideration is a bonus issue to existing members. In this case shares are issued to members in proportion to their existing holdings. If this happens the nominal value of the shares is transferred to a company's capital from its revenue reserves. This money is then part of the company's capital and not available for distribution.

Many of the procedures are the same as those for the issue of shares for a cash consideration. However, the following points should be noted:

- In the case of a public company, it is not permitted for the consideration to consist of an undertaking to do work or provide services.

- In the case of a public company, the consideration must be the subject of a valuation report conducted by an independent person. There are certain exceptions to this, including take-overs and share exchanges where the offer is available to all holders of that class of share.

- There are tight rules about the contents of the independent valuer's report, how it is presented, and the qualifications and independence of the valuer.

- There should normally be a formal agreement, approved by the directors, in respect of the non-cash consideration.

- This agreement must be stamped in accordance with Inland Revenue regulations and submitted to the Registrar of Companies, accompanied by form 88(2). If the agreement is not in writing, form 88(3) must be submitted to the Registrar of Companies.

The issue of shares at a premium

This occurs when shares are sold at a price in excess of their nominal value. It is permissible for this to be done and the premium may either be cash or non-cash, but the amount of the premium must be credited to a separate share premium account. This forms part of the capital reserves and may not be distributed in the same way as revenue reserves.

Section 130 of the Act provides that the share premium account may only be used for the following purposes:

- To write off preliminary expenses.

- To pay the expenses of an issue of shares or debentures.

- To pay the commission on an issue of shares or debentures, or the discount on an issue of debentures.

- To provide a premium payable on the redemption of debentures.

- To pay up unissued shares to be allotted to members as fully paid.

However, Sections 130 to 134 of the Act provide relief from these requirements in certain defined circumstances relating to mergers and group reconstructions. If not used in one of the permitted ways, the share premium account must be retained as part of the capital of the company.

The issue of shares at a discount

This occurs when shares are sold at a price less than their nominal value. The issuing of shares at a discount is not permitted by the Act, and it is a criminal offence for the company and any officers involved. Furthermore, the person allotted the shares may be compelled to pay to the company the amount of the discount plus interest.

It is lawful for a company to pay a commission of up to ten per cent in respect of the issue of shares. The issue of debentures at a discount is permitted.

Pre-emption rights

There is a general requirement under the Act that new shares to be issued for cash must be offered to existing shareholders in proportion to their existing holdings. Only shares not accepted by the existing shareholders may be allotted to non-shareholders. This is what is meant by pre-emption. The principle and details of this are covered by Sections 89 to 96 of the Act. Pre-emption rights apply to shares, securities that may be converted into shares and options to acquire shares. Pre-emption rights do **NOT** apply to:

- Subscribers' and bonus shares

- Shares allotted under an employees' share scheme

- Shares with limited rights as to dividends and capital participation

- Shares allotted, wholly or partially, for non-cash consideration.

The offer to existing shareholders must be made in writing to members' registered addresses, and the offer must remain open for at least 21 days. Only when the offer period has expired, or non-acceptance has been communicated to the company, may shares be otherwise allotted.

The memorandum or articles of a private company may override statutory provisions concerning pre-emption rights. A private company's memorandum or articles may exclude pre-emption rights, or may stipulate that they operate in detail in a way different from the Act's requirements.

In both public and private companies pre-emption rights may be modified or abolished, if directors have been given a general authorisation under Section 80 to allot shares. Such authorisation may have been given by the articles or by a special resolution of the members.

There are certain requirements of listed companies relating to pre-emption rights.

Financial assistance and the acquisition of a company's shares

Subject to certain exceptions it is, in general, not lawful for either a public company or a private company to give financial assistance to help in the acquisition of its own shares. The definition of financial assistance is widely drawn and includes, for example, gifts, loans, indemnities, etc. Section 151 of the Act states in part.

> *'...It is not lawful for the company or any of its subsidiaries to give financial assistance directly or indirectly for the purpose of that acquisition before or at the same time as the acquisition takes place.'*

Section 153(3) of the Act provides a long list of exceptions. These include (among others) a loan by a company that gives loans in the normal course of its business, such as a bank, the providing of money in connection with an employees' share scheme and the distribution of profits by a lawful dividend.

Private companies are exempt from the prohibition if the step is sanctioned by the members by means of a special resolution and if the company's net assets are not reduced as a consequence, or, if they are reduced, the financial assistance is provided out of distributable profits. Section 155 sets out the several detailed requirements that must be met and the procedures that must be followed.

Reduction of capital

This is allowed as long as it is permitted by the articles. However, the step must be sanctioned by the members by means of a special resolution, and it must also be sanctioned by the court. A public company may not, unless exceptionally the court agrees, reduce the nominal value of its allotted share capital to a figure less than £50,000. The court may make such conditions as it sees fit.

Reduction of share capital, and in particular application to the court, is rather technical and professional assistance may well be required. The court will be concerned to safeguard the interests of creditors. In most circumstances creditors must receive notice of the application to the court, and have a chance to make representations to it. When court approval has been received, the Registrar of Companies must be notified. This is done by sending an approved minute, showing details of the reduced capital, a copy of the court order and a copy of the memorandum altered to reflect the change. The Registrar will issue a certificate of registration and the change takes place from the date of the certificate.

Acquisition by a company of its own shares

A company is, with certain circumstances exempted, not permitted to acquire its own shares. It may only do so for certain purposes and if certain procedures are strictly followed. If the company acts in contravention of this, the company is liable to a fine and officers at fault are liable to a fine, to imprisonment or both. Furthermore, the purported acquisition of shares will be void.

Section 143 of the Act stipulates in what circumstances a company may acquire rights in its shares. Part of the section states:

'A company limited by shares may acquire any of its own fully paid shares otherwise than for valuable consideration; and subsection (1) does not apply in relation to:

a) *the redemption or purchase of shares in accordance with Chapter VII of this Part*

b) *the acquisition of shares in a reduction of capital duly made*

c) *the purchase of shares in pursuance of an order of the court under section 5 (alteration of objects) section 54 (litigated objection to resolution for company to be re-registered as private) or Part XVII (relief to members unfairly prejudiced) or*

d) *the forfeiture of shares, or the acceptance of shares surrendered in lieu, in pursuance of the articles, for failure to pay any sum payable in respect of the shares.'*

Chapter VII of the Act is headed 'Redeemable Shares; Purchases By A Company Of Its Own Shares' and consists of Sections 159 to 181. Only fully paid shares may be redeemed and the terms of redemption must provide for payment on redemption. Redeemable shares may only be issued provided that some irredeemable shares are already in issue.

A company may only purchase its own shares if authorised to do so by its articles. Purchased shares must be cancelled by the company, thus reducing the issued share capital but not the authorised share capital. Such purchases must leave some non-redeemable equity shares in issue.

Authority for a company to purchase its own shares must be given by the members by means of a special resolution, and this must be given before the purchases are made. If shares are to be purchased by private treaty, the proposed contract must be available for inspection at the meeting which votes on the special resolution and it must be available for inspection at the registered office for the 15 days prior to the meeting. If shares are to be acquired by market purchases, the special resolution must specify the minimum number of shares that may be purchased and the maximum price that may be paid. The resolution must also specify a date at which the authority expires, and this date must not be more than 18 months in the future.

Acquisition by a company of its own shares is a large subject. The above is an outline guide only and there are further considerations not covered. These include taxation, and professional guidance thereon is recommended.

Checklist

- The issue of shares must be done exactly as specified by memorandum, the articles or an ordinary resolution of the members.

- The authority to issue shares may impose conditions or it may be unconditional.

- A private company may not offer its shares to the public.

- The Registrar of Companies must be informed of details of allotment on form 88(2).

- There are extra rules for the issue of shares by a public company.

- The issue of shares for non-cash consideration is common in take-overs.

- There are tight extra rules for the issue of shares for non-cash consideration.

- Shares may be issued at a premium, but the premium must be kept separate and only used for certain purposes.

- Issue of shares at a discount is forbidden, but commission of up to 10 per cent is permitted.

- Generally, pre-emption rights must be observed, but there are exceptions. The memorandum or articles of a private company may vary the rules.

- Financial assistance to help with the purchase of a company's own shares is generally prohibited, but there are exceptions.

- Redemption of capital is allowed if it is permitted by the articles. It must be sanctioned by a special resolution of the members and by the court.

- A company may (with certain exceptions) acquire its own shares, but only for certain purposes and by following the correct procedure.

chapter eight

Debentures and loan stock

Introduction

Definitions and brief descriptions

Power to issue debentures

Fixed and floating charges

Transferability and stamp duty

Trustees

Trust deed

Registration of charges

Checklist

Introduction

It is fitting that this chapter should be located just after the chapter on share capital because debentures and loan stock can be structured in a way that make them almost an extension of share capital. It is true that fixed payments attach to them rather than equity participation, but debentures and loan stock may (subject to the terms) be convertible. The attraction for a company is that it is a source of long-term finance that, subject to the conditions, is only repayable at a fixed date or if the covenants are breached. Unless debentures or loan stock are convertible, they have the effect of increasing the gearing of the equity shares.

Debentures are also a standard form of security for bank lending and other lending. They give the holder (or lender) a fixed or floating charge (or both) over the assets of the company. Company secretaries may need to be familiar with debentures and the various technicalities, which are important. Charges must almost always be correctly registered with the Registrar of Companies. The holder's priority is jeopardised if this is not done.

Definitions and brief descriptions

The remainder of this chapter deals with various issues concerning debentures and loan stock. It is as well first of all to be familiar with the different types and this section is intended to assist the necessary understanding.

Debenture

This is a document which acknowledges or creates a debt, and promises repayment, with or without encompassing a charge or mortgage on one or more assets as security for it. Although this is a valid definition, in practice a charge or mortgage is nearly always an essential feature. The different types of debenture are explained further below. Section 744 of the Act defines a debenture as follows:

> *'includes debenture stock, bonds and any other security of a company, whether constituting a charge on the assets of the company or not'*

Registered debenture

These are much more common than bearer debentures. In the case of
a registered debenture, the holder of the debenture is registered with
the company and, subject to the articles, ownership is transferable. This
is normally done by means of a standard stock transfer form. Following
transfer, the name of the new owner is endorsed onto the debenture
and details are also entered into company records. Details of certain
types of debenture must be registered with the Registrar of Companies,
and this is covered later in this chapter.

The conditions of the loan will form part of the debenture document,
usually being printed on the rear. These terms will cover such matters
as transfer, redemption, interest, etc. Registered debentures are mainly
issued by private companies, either singly or as part of a series. They
are, though, the standard form of charge obtained by banks for lending
to both private and public companies. Such debentures often relate to
'all monies' lending.

Bearer debenture

Bearer debentures are in practice rare and unlikely to be encountered.
They are debentures where the benefits of ownership are transferable
by delivery. In this respect they are similar to share warrants to bearer.

Debenture stock

Equity stock is now encountered only rarely, but debenture stock issued
by public companies is much more common. There are many similarities with registered debentures and the issue is secured by the assets
of the company. Debenture stock may be quoted on a Stock Exchange.

The whole amount of the debenture stock issue is treated as one fund
and there will be a trust deed between the company and a trustee. Each
holder of the debenture stock will hold a certificate relating to a specified part of the whole fund.

Debenture stock is sometimes issued with convertible terms. This means
that the holder may convert them into equity shares in accordance with
the terms of the debenture stock issue. These terms will specify the times
that the conversion option may be exercised and the formula for conversion. Such conversions may be very attractive or very unattractive,
according to the fortunes of the company in the meantime. Convert-

ible debenture stock may only be issued in accordance with the rules and procedures applicable to equity capital.

Redeemable debenture stock is not common but may be encountered. If so, the trust deed will specify the terms (particularly price) and date or dates at which the company has the option of redemption. As debentures are loans and not capital, the restrictions on the repayment of capital do not apply. Redemption may be at par or with a premium.

Unsecured loan stock

The words convey the meaning very well, but the key word to note is 'unsecured'. It is not secured on the assets of the company. With this very large difference, it is very like debenture loan stock. The lack of security often means that steps have to be taken to make the issue attractive. This may be a high rate of interest or it may mean making the loan stock convertible at some future date. Or it may mean both these things. Trust deeds often provide for unsecured loan stock to be repayable if certain events occur. These might, for example, include a scheduled interest payment being overdue by a certain number of days.

Power to issue debentures

There are two separate issues:

- Do the directors have the necessary borrowing powers?

- Do the directors have the power to issue debentures?

The short answer to the first question is 'probably yes'. Trading companies have an implied power to borrow money for the purposes of the business, and this will be sufficient unless the powers are restricted by the memorandum or articles. In practice, memorandum and articles often grant specific powers, even though they are already implied. Furthermore, the wording is often very liberal concerning the powers and the purposes of the borrowing. This may be important if the purposes go beyond a strict definition of trading.

The answer to the second question is also 'very probably yes', but it will depend on the precise form and terms of the debenture and on the memorandum and articles. The terms of the trust deed (if there is one) and of the debenture must comply with any detailed restrictions which may, or may not, be in the memorandum and articles. There are many possibilities for difficulties on such matters as redemption, convertibility, etc. The directors are required to follow correct procedures when issuing debentures and these are similar to procedures for the issue of shares.

Fixed and floating charges

A fixed charge relates to a specific identified asset or specified assets. These assets are the security of the debenture holders and the directors are forbidden to dispose of them. They will probably also be required to insure them and maintain them in good order. Disposal may only be with the permission of the debenture holder or trustee.

A floating charge relates to all the assets of the company. Directors are allowed to buy and sell assets subject to a floating charge, so long as it is done in the normal course of business for the benefit of the company. The terms of a floating charge usually prevent a fixed charge being created to rank ahead of the floating charge. But it is allowed if they do not do so.

Debentures are often secured by a charge that is both fixed and floating, and bank lending is often secured in this way. This means that the bank (or other debenture holder) has a fixed charge over certain assets, possibly items such as plant and machinery, plus a floating charge over all the other assets.

Floating charges are normally structured so that they convert to fixed charges if specified events occur. Typically, these events include the passing of a winding-up resolution and the non-payment of interest after a certain number of days following the due payment date. When this happens the debenture holder may appoint a receiver and take control of the specified assets. The position is slightly different under Scottish law, where a floating charge only becomes fixed when a receiver is appointed or when winding-up commences.

A debenture holder receives priority over all other creditors in respect of the proceeds of the security attaching to it. If the security is realised it must be done with reasonable care. Any surplus, after satisfying the debenture holders in full, goes to the other creditors. It is possible to create more than one charge over the same asset, as in first and second mortgages on property. If this is done, and if registration is properly completed, the security of the second charge ranks after the security of the first charge.

Transferability and stamp duty

A company is not permitted to register the transfer of a debenture unless it has received a properly executed instrument of transfer. This means a stock transfer form that complies with the Stock Transfer Act 1963. Transfer must be in accordance with the terms of the debenture and issue.

Stamp duty on the transfer of debentures is the same as stamp duty on the transfer of shares. The transfer of loan stock is, with certain detailed exceptions, exempt from stamp duty.

Trustees

If there is a single debenture holder, such as a bank for example, there is no need for trustees. The holder will look after his own interests and take any steps that may be necessary. This is not possible when the issue is of debenture stock, and in this case it is necessary to have a trustee or trustees to look after the collective interest of the stockholders. The precise powers of the trustees will depend on the wording of the trust deed.

Trust deed

The trust deed is the key legal document setting out the rights of the parties. As its name implies it must be sealed as explained in Chapter 3, *The statutory registers and the company seal*. Wording and contents may vary, but it is likely (among other things) to include:

- Covenants by the company. These may relate either to the specific assets or to more general matters. An example of the former is to keep the assets properly insured. An example of the latter is to keep total borrowings (from all sources) below a certain figure.

- A prohibition on the issuing of another charge ranking ahead of, or equal to, a floating charge (if there is one).

- The actual charges over the specified property.

- Details of the rate of interest on the loan stock.

- Details of the issue and conversion rights (if any).

Registration of charges

Nearly all charges must be registered with the Registrar of Companies. Section 396 of the Act states that (in England and Wales) the following types of charge must be registered:

a) a charge for the purpose of securing any issue of debentures,

b) a charge on uncalled share capital of the company,

c) a charge created or evidenced by an instrument which, if executed by an individual, would require registration as a bill of sale,

d) a charge on land (wherever situated) or any interest in it, but not including a charge for any rent or other periodical sum issuing out of the land,

e) a charge on book debts of the company,

f) a floating charge on the company's undertaking or property,

g) a charge on calls made but not paid,

h) a charge on a ship or aircraft, or any share in a ship,

i) a charge on goodwill (or on any intellectual property).

As with so many things, the list is slightly different for Scotland and this may be found in Section 410 of the Act.

Registration must usually be done by means of form 395, though in some circumstances form 397a or form 400 must be used. Registration must be within 21 days of the creation of the charge. Responsibility for registering the charge lies with the company that issued it. However, registration may be conducted by any party with an interest. In practice, it is nearly always done by the trustee or the debenture holder. This is because the consequences of not doing so may be awful for them.

If a charge is not properly registered, the trustee or debenture holder will retain rights against the company and the money becomes immediately repayable. However, the charge will not be valid against a liquidator or other creditors. There may also be the possibility of criminal charges. Proper registration with the Registrar of Companies constitutes notice to all the world, and is why the appropriate records at Companies House are examined so assiduously in search of prior charges.

Checklist

- A charge or mortgage is almost always an essential feature of a debenture.

- The holder of a registered debenture is registered with the company and, subject to the articles, ownership is transferable.

- The conditions of the loan are normally printed on the rear of a registered debenture.

- Debenture stock issued by a public company is quite common and is often issued on convertible terms. Redeemable debenture stock is not common, but may be encountered.

- With unsecured loan stock, the key word is 'unsecured'. There is a lack of security and a high rate of interest may be necessary.

- For a debenture to be valid, the directors must have the necessary borrowing powers and the power to issue debentures. They probably have, but may not.

- A fixed charge relates to a specific identified asset or specified assets.

- A floating charge relates to all the assets of the company. A floating charge normally converts to a fixed charge if certain events occur – such as the passing of a winding-up resolution.

- A company may not register the transfer of a debenture unless it has received a duly stamped, properly executed instrument of transfer.

- Trustees are necessary in the case of debenture stock.

- The trust deed is the key legal document.

- Nearly all charges must be registered.

- Usually, registration is done by the debenture holder, because he has much to lose if it is not done.

chapter nine

The Memorandum of Association

Introduction

The name of the company

Registered office

The objects of the company

Other clauses in the memorandum

Subscription clause

Disclosure of information on company stationery

Checklist

Introduction

The memorandum is at the very heart of a company's constitution and it is often grouped with the articles as in the phrase 'memorandum and articles'. The articles deal with the rules for running the company, whereas the memorandum deals with its registration and relationship with the outside world. It is required to include the following:

- The name of the company.

- The fact that it is a public company, if this is the case.

- The country in which the registered office is to be situated.

- The objects of the company.

- The fact that the liability of members is limited, if this is the case.

- The amount of the authorised share capital and its division into shares of a fixed amount, if the company has a share capital.

The memorandum concludes with a subscription clause. It is required that the memorandum be as close to the correct statutory form as individual circumstances allow. This is Table B for private companies and Table F for public companies.

There is a requirement that a copy of the memorandum and articles must, on request, be sent to any member. A charge of up to 5p may be made which is hardly likely to wreck company finances. Any changes that have been made must be incorporated into the copy that is sent. It must include (or be accompanied by) any resolutions of the company which were required to be filed with the Registrar of Companies.

The name of the company

A company may choose to use different trading names but there can only be one registered name, and this is the name given in the first clause of its memorandum. It is possible to amend the memorandum and this is explained later. If the company is a private limited company, the name must end with 'Ltd' or 'Limited'. If the company is a public limited company, the name must end with 'PLC' or 'Public Limited Company'. The equivalent Welsh language words and abbreviations are permitted.

The correct, full name of the company must be clearly and legibly displayed in the following places:

- Outside every office and all business premises of the company.

- On the company seal, if the company has one.

- On all business letters and certain company documents. This is covered more fully later in this chapter.

The memorandum may say that the company's registered office will be located in Wales, rather than the more usual 'in England and Wales'. If this is the case, certain special rules apply. These relate to the use of the Welsh language and are optional, not compulsory.

There are over 1,500,000 companies registered with the Registrar of Companies and each registered name is unique. It is therefore easy to appreciate why rules for registration exist, and why some control over the choice of a company name is necessary. The Registrar (acting on the authority of the Secretary of State) may reject a proposed name on any of the following grounds:

- It is identical to the name of a company already registered. So it will not be possible to have 'Marks and Spencer PLC'.

- It is too similar to the name of a company already registered. It is easy to state the principle, but detailed application can cause much debate. However, it is safe to assume that 'Marks and Spencers PLC' would not be acceptable. This may be very unfortunate if a Mr Marks and a Mr Spencers are both proud of their names and wish to start a business. 'Spencers and Marks' might or might not be acceptable.

- It does not end with the correct designation of 'Ltd', 'Limited', 'PLC' or 'Public Limited Company'.

- It is offensive. This, too, can cause endless debate. As this guide is intended to be easily accessible no examples will be given.

- It constitutes a criminal offence.

- It gives the impression that the company is connected with central or local government. So 'Kent County Council Dustbin Emptiers Ltd' would almost certainly be rejected.

- It contains a word classed as 'sensitive' and the necessary consent has not been given. The body from whom consent must be obtained varies according to the word. Examples of such words are 'National', 'Society', 'Charity' and 'University'.

There may be dangers in the use of a company name, even if it has been successfully registered as part of the memorandum or successfully altered. Company secretaries should be aware of the potential problems, and be aware that it is wise to make checks and to try to anticipate pitfalls. The three main potential problems are:

- A name may infringe a registered trade mark.

- An established business, not necessarily a company, may bring an action for 'passing off'. This may succeed if there is a risk of confusion. It is not necessary to register business names and it can be difficult to establish the facts.

- The Registrar may require a name to be altered, even though it has been accepted for registration. This may be on the grounds that it is too similar to a name on the register or that should already have been on the register. The Registrar's power may be exercised within one year, but within five years if he has been misled by the company. In practice, he is only likely to act if a complaint is made.

A company may choose to conduct its business in a name different from the one registered by its memorandum. Such a name may not be registered but certain rules and restrictions apply. In particular, there are rules concerning the display of names at offices and other places of business, and on company stationery. The laws about passing off and registered trade marks apply to business names as well as to registered company names.

A company may elect to change its name by means of a special resolution of its members. The same checks and restrictions apply as on the first name of a company specified in the memorandum. The change of name takes legal effect from the date of the issue by the Registrar of the certificate of incorporation on change of name. This happens on a large scale with so called 'off the shelf companies'. These are registered in usually rather bland names by company formation agents and then sold on.

When the certificate of incorporation on change of name has been issued a company must:

- alter all company leaflets, stationery, etc to show the new name correctly;

- file a copy of the revised memorandum at Companies House; and

- if the company uses a seal, obtain a new seal.

Registered office

The memorandum must make it clear that the registered office will be situated in one of three areas:

- England and Wales.

- Wales.

- Scotland.

The location of the registered office determines whether English law or Scottish law will apply to the company. In the first two cases English law applies and in the third case it is Scottish law. Jersey, Guernsey, the Isle of Man and Northern Ireland are not in Great Britain and have their own registries. They are outside the scope of this guide.

In practice Companies House will accept just 'England'. This has the same legal effect as 'England and Wales'.

If the registered office is registered as 'in Wales', certain rules apply about company documents and the use of the Welsh language. These are optional, not compulsory.

The first registered office is specified on form 10 which must accompany the registration documents. The address of the registered office may be altered by a decision of the directors and the Registrar of Companies must be notified of such a change by means of form 287. The change only takes effect when it is registered by the Registrar. For a period of 14 days from the date of registration, delivery to the previous registered office constitutes valid delivery or service of a document.

The registered office must be situated within the territory specified in the memorandum. It may for example be changed from London to Liverpool (if it is registered in England and Wales), but not from London to Glasgow.

There are many practical reasons for wishing to change the address of a registered office. A common one is the fact that it influences the tax district that deals with a company's affairs and a change in the address of the registered office may result in better relations with the Inland Revenue. There is no requirement that a company's registered office be a trading office. For example, an accountant's office or solicitor's office may be chosen.

Delivery to a company's registered office constitutes valid service of legal documents. This is so if they do not receive early attention, if they are lost by the post clerk, if the office is closed for the annual holiday, and even if it is a solicitor's office and the solicitor neglects to pass them on to his client. A company cannot 'go away' from its registered office even if this is what it actually does. A company must have a registered office and an existing office continues until the company goes through the correct procedure to change it.

There are provisions for the case of a company registered in Scotland but carrying on business in England or Wales. A document may be served by delivery to the principal English office and addressed to the Manager. If this is done a copy must be sent to the Scottish registered office by post.

The objects of the company

The words 'objects clause' are likely to induce boredom in many readers. Case law has a long history of tedious disputes about whether actions have been beyond the scope of an objects clause and therefore ultra vires.

The origin of the objects clause was the reasonable need to assure members that a company would only spend their money in ways for which advance permission had been given. A company set up with the object of selling top hats in Venezuela could not suddenly spend shareholders' money mending gas ovens in Bognor Regis. Directors that acted ultra vires did so at their peril. There were also risks for people who contracted with the company or who lent money to it. This was based on the principle that a memorandum registered at Companies House is notice to all the world.

Problems concerning objects clauses are now much less common than was formerly the case. There are three principal reasons for this:

- It became the custom for objects clauses to be extremely long and extremely widely drawn. Furthermore, each object was stated to be independent of the others. This meant that virtually anything was within the objects of the company. It also defeated the purpose of having an objects clause in the first place.

- Under the Companies Act 1989 it is possible to register to carry on the business of a general commercial company. This gives the directors authority to do all such things as are incidental or conducive to the carrying on of any trade or business of the company. It will not, though, give the directors powers to do things beyond this definition.

- Under the Companies Act 1989 an act of the company cannot be ultra vires, as far as a third party is concerned, because of the objects clause in its memorandum. This means that a third party can enforce contracts made by the company. However, the acts of an agent may be ultra vires if they are not within the scope of the objects clause. This protection does not extend to directors' responsibilities to members. They may be personally liable if they act ultra vires.

A company may alter its objects clause by means of a special resolution. Notice of the meeting must be sent to debenture holders and to the holders of non-voting shares as well as to the holders of voting shares. A certified copy of the resolution must be sent to the Registrar within 15 days of the passing of the resolution.

After such a resolution has been passed, application may be made to the court to have it cancelled. This must be done within 21 days and must be done by the holders of 15 per cent of the nominal value of the company's shares, or of 15 per cent of the nominal value of any class of its shares. There are other categories of people entitled to apply but these are unlikely to be encountered in practice. The Registrar must be informed if an application to the court is made and he must be notified of the outcome.

A printed copy of the altered memorandum must be delivered to the Registrar. If no application has been made to the court, this must be done within 36 days of the passing of the resolution. If application is made to the court and the court confirms the change, a printed copy of the memorandum must be delivered to the Registrar within 15 days of the court's decision, or such longer period as the court may allow.

Other clauses in the memorandum

Public company

If the company is a public company, this must stated in the memorandum. This is what governs whether the company is a public company or a private company. There are, of course, many consequences.

Limited liability

If the liability of the members is limited, the memorandum must contain a clause to this effect.

The amount of the authorised share capital

If the company has a share capital, the memorandum must state the total authorised amount of the share capital and how it is divided into shares of fixed amounts.

Subscription clause

The memorandum must be subscribed (signed) by at least two people if it is a public company, but just one person is sufficient if it is a private company. More people may subscribe if it is so wished. Subscribers may be companies or other bodies, in which case an authorised person should sign on their behalf. Subscribers may take any number of shares, provided that the total does not exceed the authorised share capital.

Subscribers are automatically members of the company and therefore no formal allotment of shares is necessary. Subscribers must pay for their shares, but if the company allots the whole of its authorised share capital to other people who are liable to pay for the shares, the subscribers need not pay. Subscribers for shares in a public company must pay for their shares in cash. Non-cash consideration is not acceptable.

Disclosure of information on company stationery

Readers will be aware that the obligations do not meet with universal compliance, and that there is considerable ignorance about what is required. Omissions and inaccuracies are an offence, and in some circumstances there is a risk of individuals incurring personal liability. This may happen if a person contracts with a company in the reasonable belief that limited liability does not apply. Failure to disclose company details on notepaper may be a strong factor in that belief. The requirements relating to company notepaper and order forms are as follows:

- The company's full, correct name must be shown.

- The company's place of registration must be shown. This is England and Wales, England, Wales or Scotland. Alternatively, it is acceptable to put 'registered in Cardiff' or 'registered in Edinburgh'.

- The company's registered number as shown on the certificate of incorporation must be shown.

- The address of the registered office must be shown and it must be indicated that this is the registered office.

The above applies to all companies. The following have more limited application:

- If the company is an investment company, then this fact must be disclosed. An investment company is defined by Section 266 of the Act.

- Certain companies need not use the word 'Limited' or the abbreviation 'Ltd' as part of their name. If they are limited companies, this fact must be disclosed.

- If the company is a registered charity, its charity registered number must be stated, together with the fact that it is a registered charity.

- It is not obligatory to give details of the company's share capital and the practice is very unusual. However, if reference is so made, details must be given of paid-up share capital. This requirement relates to printed details on notepaper, etc, not to the contents of a letter.

It is not a requirement that the names or nationalities of directors be shown. However, if details are given for one director, details must be given for all directors. A person signing a letter with his designatory title (eg R. L. Brown – Managing Director) does not mean that full directors' details need be shown.

The statutory information is usually shown in small print at the foot of company notepaper but this is not a requirement.

The company's full, correct name (but not necessarily the other details) must be shown on all notices and other official publications of the company, bills of exchange, promissory notes, endorsements, cheques, orders for money or goods purporting to be signed by or on behalf of the company, bills of parcels, invoices, receipts and letters of credit.

Checklist

- A copy of the memorandum must, on request, be sent to any member.

- Every incorporated company has one unique registered name.

- It is possible to amend most parts of the memorandum.

- The correct, full name of the company must be displayed outside every company office, on business stationery and on the company seal, if there is one.

- The location of the registered office determines whether English law or Scottish law applies.

- The name may not be too similar to the name of another registered company, and there are other restrictions.

- It is prudent to make enquiries about possible problems with a name, and to do so before registration.

- Delivery of a document to a company's registered office constitutes good service.

- A company must have a registered office and cannot 'go away' from it. The directors can (within the same country) change the address of the registered office.

- An act of the company cannot now, because of the objects clause in the memorandum, be ultra vires vis à vis an outsider acting in good faith.

- Directors may be personally liable to shareholders if they act outside the scope of the objects clause in the memorandum.

- There are several requirements relating to information that must be shown on company stationery. Full details are in this chapter.

- It is dangerous not to show the required information on company stationery. It is an offence and can result in personal liability.

chapter ten

Articles of Association

Introduction

Model sets of articles

Freedom to adopt articles

Registration procedure and required
format of articles

Alteration of articles

Table A for a company limited by shares

Table C for a company limited by guarantee

Checklist

Introduction

This is one of the most important chapters in this guide. The Articles of Association are the internal rules by which a company is governed. They are important to all company officers, not least the company secretary. Over a period the company secretary is bound to be asked many detailed questions concerning the internal constitution of the company. Examples of such questions are:

- We have been asked to issue a duplicate share certificate. Are we allowed to do it?

- What is the approved wording for a proxy vote?

- The Sales Director has claimed £500 expenses for his wife to attend the Christmas party. Do we have to pay?

- The chairman refuses to call a Board Meeting. What can the other directors do about it?

The answers to these and other questions may well be in the articles.

A copy of the articles, together with the memorandum, must be supplied to any member on request. A fee of 5p may be charged.

Model sets of articles

The various main Companies Acts have contained or been accompanied by specimen sets of articles for the different types of companies. Regulations in connection with the Companies Act 1985 contain the following:

- Table A for a company limited by shares.

- Table C for a company limited by guarantee (without a share capital).

- Table D for a public company limited by guarantee (with a share capital).

- Table E for an unlimited company (with a share capital).

Approximately 96% of all British companies are limited by shares and approximately 3.5 % of all British companies are limited by guarantee. The latest Table A is reproduced in Appendix A and the latest Table C is reproduced in Appendix B.

The scope of a company to adopt the model articles is explained in the next section.

Freedom to adopt articles

A company is free to choose to adopt the applicable table from the above list. Tables such as these have been contained in each of the main Companies Acts, notably 1985, 1948, 1929 and even earlier, or in regulations issued in connection with then. A company that adopts one of the tables adopts the articles (table) in force at the time. This means, for example, that a company incorporated in 1951 that chose Table A would have adopted Table A from the Companies Act 1948.

Such a company would still be bound by Table A of the Companies Act 1948, unless the company had taken positive action to change to a later Table A. Confusion is possible and company secretaries should consider the desirability of making such a change. Of course, specific legislation has in some cases overridden particular articles from earlier tables. Specific legislation takes precedence and an example is the Companies Act 1985 (Electronic Communications) Order 2000.

There is no compulsion for a company to adopt Table A or one of the other tables. It may adopt a completely different set of articles. This is more likely to happen in the case of public companies with particular needs, and they often adopt so-called 'long-form' articles. A common reason for not adopting Table A in its entirety is a wish to restrict the transferability of shares. The options of all companies are:

* Adopt Table A (or one of the other tables) in its entirety.

* Reject Table A (and the other tables) and adopt a specially written set of articles.

* Adopt part of Table A (or one of the other tables) but not all of it, and adopt additional specially written articles. In practice this is the option chosen for the majority of companies.

Table A (or one of the other tables) is deemed to apply unless it has been specifically rejected, or is inconsistent with articles that have been adopted. The Stock Exchange requires the articles of listed companies to meet certain criteria.

Registration procedure and required format of articles

Section 7(3) of the Act states:

'Articles must:

a) be printed

b) be divided into paragraphs numbered consecutively, and

c) be signed by each subscriber of the memorandum in the presence of at least one witness who must attest the signature'

It will be noted that both Table A and Table C have consecutively numbered paragraphs.

The articles must be lodged with the Registrar for registration. However, a company limited by shares may adopt Table A, and may do so without modification. In this case no articles need be supplied, Table A will apply automatically and the memorandum will be endorsed to indicate that the company was registered without articles. A company that adopts one of Tables C, D or E must register the articles, even if they are identical with one of the tables. The different treatment is an apparent anomaly and it seems reasonable to suspect that MPs were not concentrating at the relevant time.

The articles, when registered, bind the company and all the members individually. The same is true of the memorandum.

Alteration of articles

Section 9 of the Act provides that, subject to the provisions of the Act and to the conditions of the memorandum, a company may alter its articles by special resolution. Provided that the technicalities are correctly observed, this may be done at any time and on any scale. An alteration may be of a minor detail in one article, or it may be a complete substitution of a different set of articles.

A copy of the new articles must be signed as verification of its authenticity, and this is usually done by the chairman of the meeting that passed the special resolution, but it may be done by any company officer, including the Company Secretary. This certified copy must be sent to the Registrar of Companies within 15 days of the resolution being passed. If the alteration is very short and clear, a suitably signed and altered copy may be sent to the Registrar. If this is not the case, a complete set of altered articles must be sent. If in doubt, it is recommended that this course be adopted.

It can happen in practice that internal confusion arises later over what exactly are the latest articles. This should not happen, and usually does not happen, but it is more likely when there have been many changes. Company secretaries should take care to keep precise records of the changes and have copies of the latest articles available.

Table A for a company limited by shares

The current Table A regulations to the Companies Act 1985 are reproduced in full in Appendix A to this guide. The following points may be of particular interest to company secretaries. **The points are abbreviated and summarised. Reference to table A is recommended.**

Share capital (regs. 2 to 5)

- Redeemable shares may be issued.

- The company shall not recognise any person as holding a share on trust.

Calls on shares and forfeiture (regs. 12 to 22)

- Calls may be made by the directors.

- Interest is payable in the case of late payment.

- Shares may be forfeited in the case of non-payment.

Transfer of shares (regs. 23 to 28)

- The instrument of transfer may be in any form approved by the directors.

Purchase of own shares (reg. 35)

- Purchase of a company's own shares is permitted.

Notice of general meetings (regs. 38 and 39)

- 21 days notice is necessary for an Annual General Meeting, and for an Extraordinary General Meeting called for the passing of a special resolution or a resolution appointing a person as a director. Shorter notice is possible in some circumstances.

Proceedings at general meetings (regs. 40 to 53)

- A quorum must be present and this consists of two people entitled to vote.

- There are procedures to deal with the absence of a quorum.

- The meeting may be adjourned.

- Votes will be decided on a show of hands unless a poll is demanded.

Votes of members (regs. 54 to 63)

- On a show of hands, each member has one vote.

- In a poll, each member has one vote for each share held.

- Votes may not be cast in respect of shares on which money is owing to the company.

- In a poll, votes may be made personally or by proxy.

Number of directors (reg. 64)

- There must be at least two (unless otherwise determined by an ordinary resolution). There is no maximum figure.

Alternate directors (regs. 65 to 69)

- Any director may, subject to the detailed requirements, appoint an alternate director.

Powers of directors (regs. 70 to 71)

- Subject to the Act, the memorandum, the articles and any directions given by special resolution, the directors may exercise all of the powers of the company.

Delegation of directors' powers (reg. 72)

- The directors may delegate their powers to any of their number singly or in combination. This may be subject to such conditions as they see fit.

Appointment and retirement of directors (regs. 73 to 80)

- At the first Annual General Meeting all directors shall retire.

- At subsequent Annual General Meetings one third of directors shall retire.

- Retiring directors may be reappointed.

- Directors may fill a casual vacancy or appoint an additional director.

Directors' appointments and interests (regs. 84 to 86)

- Subject to the provisions of the Act, the directors may make one of their number managing director and may make appointments to all executive offices.

- Subject to the provisions of the Act, and provided that he has made full disclosure to the other directors, a director may benefit from a transaction with the company.

Proceedings of directors (regs. 88 to 98)

- Subject to the articles, the directors may regulate their proceedings as they think fit.

- Any director may call a meeting of the directors. The company secretary must call a meeting of the directors if so requested by a director.

- The quorum for a meeting of directors is two, unless the directors fix a different figure.

- The directors may appoint one of their number to be chairman and they may remove him from that office.

- Unless the articles provide otherwise, a director may not vote on a matter in which he has a material interest. There are certain specified exceptions.

Secretary (reg. 99)

- The company secretary shall be appointed by the directors, and may be removed by them.

Minutes (reg. 100)

- Minutes shall be kept. This means minutes of all general meetings, class meetings, board meetings and meetings of committees of the board.

The seal (reg. 101)

- The company seal shall only be used on the authority of the directors, or a committee of the directors.

Dividends (regs. 102 to 108)

- No dividend shall be greater than the amount recommended by the directors.

- Interim dividends may be declared and paid by the directors.

- Final dividends shall be authorised by an ordinary resolution of the members.

Notices (regs. 111 to 126)

- Any notice must be in writing, with the exception of a notice calling a meeting of the directors. Subject to certain conditions electronic communication is permitted.

- Proof that an envelope containing a notice was properly addressed, prepaid and posted shall be conclusive evidence that the notice was given.

Table C for a company limited by guarantee

The current Table C regulations to the Companies Act 1985 are reproduced in full in Appendix B to this book.

A superficial glance at Tables A and C may well lead company secretaries to the conclusion that Table C is much easier to use than Table A. This is because Table C is much shorter than Table A. Such a conclusion would be understandable but mistaken. Table C is shorter because Table A applies to a company limited by guarantee to the extent that it is not modified by Table C. Table A is a stand-alone document but if a company is limited by guarantee, it is necessary to consult both Table C and Table A.

The following points may be of particular interest to company secretaries. **The points are abbreviated and summarised. Reference to Table C is recommended.**

Members (regs. 3 and 4)

- The directors must approve the admission of new members and have a veto.

- The directors may require applicants for membership of the company to deliver an application in such form as the directors may choose.

- Members may always withdraw from membership by giving seven clear days notice to the company.

- Membership is not transferable.

- Membership ceases on death.

Votes of Members (reg. 8)

- It is always one member one vote.

Checklist

- A company may adopt the relevant table if it so wishes.

- If the relevant table is adopted, it will be the relevant table from the Companies Act in force at the time. For example, a company registered in 1951 will have the relevant table from the Companies Act 1948.

- Company secretaries should consider changing the articles so that the latest relevant table applies.

- A company does not have to use the relevant table. It can register specially-written articles, or it can partly use the relevant table and partly use specially-written articles.

- The relevant table is deemed to apply unless it is inconsistent with a particular, specially-written article.

- Articles for registration must be printed, divided into sequentially numbered paragraphs and signed by each subscriber of the memorandum.

- Any or all of the articles may be altered by a special resolution of the members.

- Company secretaries should keep precise records of changes and have copies of altered articles available.

- The latest Table A and the latest Table C are reproduced as Appendices A and B to this book. It is worth spending a little time studying them.

chapter eleven

General meetings

Introduction

The Annual General Meeting

An Extraordinary General Meeting

Resolutions and notice of resolutions

Elective regime

Single-member companies

Convening and requisitioning of meetings

Period of notice and entitlement to receive notice

Notice sent by means of electronic communication

Details and contents of notice

Proxies

Quorum

Adjournment

The chairman

Voting

Minutes

Electronic general meetings

Checklist

Introduction

It is by voting at a general meeting that members exercise ultimate control over their company. It is from this action that all devolved power is derived. At one extreme, a meeting may be a husband and wife discussing the family business at the dining room table. At the other extreme, it is thousands of people gathered in a vast centre. Such gatherings are very expensive to stage and are a major challenge to the abilities of the company secretary and the other organisers.

Theoretically the meetings of some companies could need to accommodate a million or more people, which is obviously impossible. Fortunately it does not happen in practice. Cynics note that large attendances are more likely when the business includes a well-publicised, controversial item such as directors' bonuses, or incorporates free hospitality and samples of company products.

Parliament has recognised that the members of private companies should have the right to dispense with Annual General Meetings, and this is explained in the section of this chapter headed 'elective regime'. Such a decision must be unanimous and there are safeguards. In practice it is only applicable to small private companies.

Mastery of the law and practice of general meetings is a key part of the company secretary's job. He will be involved in the planning and it is usually to him that the directors turn when an awkward question arises. This chapter starts with the different types of meeting and the different types of resolution. It moves on to the convening of meetings and the required periods of notice. The final part of the chapter deals with the correct conduct of meetings.

The Annual General Meeting

A private company may, under the elective regime, resolve not to hold Annual General Meetings. With this exception, every company must hold an Annual General Meeting as follows:

- The first Annual General Meeting must be held within 18 months of incorporation.

- An Annual General Meeting must be held in each calendar year.

- An Annual General Meeting must be held not more than 15 months after the last Annual General Meeting.

Both the second and third requirements must be met. This means, for example, that it is not permitted to hold an Annual General Meeting on 7 April, and then hold the next Annual General Meeting on 7 August, 16 months later. It is also not permitted to hold an Annual General Meeting on 3rd December and then hold the next Annual General Meeting on 3rd January, 13 months later. It should be noted that only one Annual General Meeting may be held in any one calendar year.

A meeting is the Annual General Meeting if it is described as such in the notice that convenes it. The normal business of an Annual General Meeting is as follows:

- Consideration of the accounts and reports.

- Declaration of a final dividend, if one is to be paid.

- Appointment or reappointment of the auditors and the fixing of their remuneration. In practice it is usually resolved that the remuneration be fixed by the directors.

- The election or re-election of directors.

It is possible for other business to be conducted at an annual general meeting in order to reduce the expense and trouble of calling separate meetings. If this is done, the correct formalities concerning notice and voting must be observed.

An Annual General Meeting must be held within the prescribed time limits even if audited accounts are not ready, the appointment or re-appointment of auditors does not take place and it is not appropriate to declare a final dividend. These matters may be left to the next Annual General Meeting or they may be dealt with at an Extraordinary General Meeting.

Alternatively, the Annual General Meeting may be formally opened and adjourned until a date when the accounts and reports are ready.

An Extraordinary General Meeting

Any general meeting of the members that is not an Annual General Meeting is an Extraordinary General Meeting. Any number of Extraordinary General Meetings may be held and they may be called at any time.

The purpose of an Extraordinary General Meeting is to transact special business (which is not the same as a special resolution). At an Extraordinary General Meeting resolutions may only be passed of which correct notice has been given in the notice convening the meeting.

It may sometimes be necessary to hold a meeting for the holders of just one class of share. This need may occur if something is proposed that affects their rights.

Resolutions and notice of resolutions

The different types of resolution and the required notice are considered below. The Act provides that certain resolutions must be extraordinary resolutions or special resolutions, and it also provides that special notice must be given of certain ordinary resolutions. Company articles may make the requirements more rigorous than the Act, but they cannot override the Act and make them less rigorous.

Extraordinary resolution

An extraordinary resolution must be passed with a majority of at least 75 per cent of those voting. Votes not cast are disregarded for this purpose. So, if 100 votes may be cast, 60 are cast in favour, 20 are cast against and 20 are not cast, an extraordinary resolution will be carried.

21 clear days notice must be given of an extraordinary resolution to be proposed at an Annual General Meeting. 14 clear days notice must be given of an extraordinary resolution to be proposed at an Extraordinary General Meeting. The notice must give the exact wording of the resolution and must state that it is to be proposed as an extraordinary resolution.

There are not many actions that require the sanction of an extraordinary resolution. They include:

- To voluntarily wind up the company on the grounds that it cannot meet its liabilities.

- In the case of a voluntary winding up, to sanction the use of certain powers by a liquidator.

- To vary the rights of a class of shares.

Special resolution

A special resolution must be passed with a majority of at least 75 per cent of those voting. Votes not cast are disregarded for this purpose. So, if 100 votes may be cast, 60 are cast in favour, 20 are cast against and 20 are not cast, a special resolution will be carried.

21 clear days notice must be given of a special resolution, and this is so whether it is to be proposed at an Annual General Meeting or at an Extraordinary General Meeting. The notice must give the exact wording of the resolution and must state that it is to be proposed as a special resolution.

The Act provides quite a long list of actions that must be sanctioned by a special resolution. They include:

- To voluntarily wind up a solvent company.

- To ratify an ultra vires act by the directors.

- To approve redemption of the company's shares.

- To change the company's name.

- To alter the memorandum or articles.

Elective resolution

This requires 100 per cent approval of those entitled to vote and relaxes certain specified requirements relating to meetings. A resolution to cancel an elective resolution may be passed with a simple majority of those voting. Details are given in the section of this chapter relating to the 'elective regime', and in both cases 21 clear days notice to the members is required.

Ordinary resolution

An ordinary resolution is passed with a simple majority of those voting, disregarding those entitled to vote but who do not do so. So, if 100 are present, 41 vote in favour and 39 vote against, an ordinary resolution will be carried.

Requirements concerning notice are set out elsewhere in this chapter.

An ordinary resolution is sufficient in all cases where the Act or company articles do not specify a requirement for an extraordinary resolution or a special resolution. However, in some cases special notice is required and this is explained below.

The Act specifies that a director may be removed by an ordinary resolution, though special notice is required. The Act also specifies that an auditor may be removed by an ordinary resolution, and this too requires special notice. Company articles may not override these provisions.

Special notice of an ordinary resolution

This only relates to certain ordinary resolutions and does not affect the way in which they may be passed by a simple majority as described above.

Special notice must be given to the company at least 28 days before the meeting at which the resolution is to be proposed. This may be done by any member, regardless of the size of his shareholding. The company must then give notice to the members of the resolution. This is normally done with the notice of the meeting. However, it may be done separately as long as members receive 21 clear days notice. In practice, it is usually done for items for a forthcoming Annual General Meeting.

The above does not give a member an unfettered right to have items put on an agenda and special notice given. It only happens if the directors agree or if the articles give the member the right to have an item included. It may be that a certain proportion of the members or shares are required.

Section 379 of the Act requires special notice of the following resolutions to be given:

- To appoint (or reappoint) a director who is over the age limit. This applies only to public companies or companies that are subsidiaries of public companies.

- To remove a director before the expiry of his period of office.

- To remove an auditor before his period of office has expired. Also to appoint a new auditor before the expiry of the period of office of an auditor, to re-appoint an auditor who was appointed by the directors to fill a casual vacancy, or to fill a casual vacancy in the position of auditor.

Written resolution

This is available to private companies only. Subject to certain restrictions, a written resolution is valid if it is signed by every member entitled to attend general meetings and vote. In practice the 100 per cent requirement limits its use to relatively small companies.

A written resolution takes effect from the date that the last signature is delivered to the company. The directors, if they are aware of the terms of the proposed written resolution, are required to give details to the auditor at the time, or before, it is sent to the first member for signature.

A written resolution may not be used to remove a director before the expiry of his term of office. Neither may it be used to remove an auditor prior to the expiry of his term of office.

Elective regime

The elective regime is a step towards deregulation. It was established by the Companies Act 1989 and is only available to private companies, including a private company that is a subsidiary of a public company. It is a recognition that the full panoply of Companies Act procedures relating to meetings may not be necessary or desirable in all cases. This is particularly so when a company has few members and they are all happy with the way that the company is being run. The elective regime is a way of lifting some of the burdens and costs.

The most widely-used concession of the elective regime is authority to dispense with Annual General Meetings. It also permits acts without sanction of a general meeting relating to certain specified actions. An abbreviated summary of what may be permitted is as follows:

• The company may dispense with the holding of Annual General Meetings.

• The directors may be given authority to allot shares indefinitely, or for a period longer than the normal five year period.

• The obligation to lay accounts and reports before members may be lifted. This does not remove the obligation to prepare accounts and reports and to send them to members.

• The auditors may be automatically reappointed.

• The majority needed to authorise short notice of an Extraordinary General Meeting may be reduced from 95 per cent to any proportion above 90 per cent.

Elective resolutions may be passed on any or all of the above matters. It does not have to be all of them. It should be particularly noted that the consent of members is still required, but that consent may be expressed in a different way. Similarly, the requirements relating to accounts, audits, etc are not changed, but the requirements relating to their consideration at meetings are relaxed.

Not holding Annual General Meetings may present one or two practical problems, but they are problems that directors (no doubt soundly advised by company secretaries) can overcome. Two such problems, and possible solutions, are as follows:

• A final dividend may only be declared by the members in a general meeting. A solution to this is not to have a final dividend, just one or more interim dividends declared by the directors.

• Directors retiring by rotation may be reappointed by the members at an Annual General Meeting. A solution to this is to change the articles so that directors do not retire by rotation, but instead serve until they resign or are removed.

It should be remembered that written resolutions are available to companies and avoid the need to hold a meeting. A written resolution requires 100 per cent support.

A resolution may only be passed as an elective resolution if it has the unanimous support of every member entitled to attend and vote. The safeguard is that it may be blocked by a single member holding a single share. 21 clear days notice must be given of an elective resolution and the notice must state that it is to be proposed as an elective resolution. The Registrar of Companies must be provided with copies of all elective resolutions and this must be done within 15 days of the passing of such a resolution.

Once passed, an elective resolution will continue in force until it is cancelled. This may be done by means of an ordinary resolution to cancel an elective resolution requiring a simple majority. An elective resolution is automatically cancelled if a private company re-registers as a public company. The Registrar of Companies must be provided with copies of all resolutions that revoke elective resolutions and this must be done within 15 days of the passing of such a resolution.

There are obvious dangers and an important safeguard should be mentioned. Within 28 days of the accounts and reports being sent out, any member (even one holding a single share) or the auditors may require a general meeting to be held for the purpose of laying the accounts and reports before the company.

Single-member companies

Single-member private companies are now permitted and this obviously defeats the concept of members meeting together to make decisions. Such companies sometimes incorporate provisions in their articles to deal with the obvious complications.

Whether or not specially adapted articles are in place, one person present in person or by proxy may constitute a general meeting. Despite this, the formalities of calling the meeting and recording decisions must be complied with. Alternatively, it is simpler to deal with business by means of written resolutions, or of course the option of the elective regime is available.

Convening and requisitioning of meetings

It is normal for the directors to convene both Annual General Meetings and Extraordinary General Meetings. It is the duty of the directors to ensure the smooth running of the company and it is normally in their interests to convene extraordinary general meetings to meet the wishes of members. Usually there is no conflict, but the directors may well convene a meeting on request, even though not compelled to do so. The directors are required to convene Annual General Meetings in accordance with the Act.

The Department of Trade and Industry may direct that a meeting be convened or may do so itself, and it may exercise these powers if requested by a member. The court also has wide powers to call a meeting.

Powers exist for members themselves to require a meeting to be held. This is the power to requisition a meeting, and it may be exercised by one or more members holding at least 10 per cent of the paid up share capital. In the case of a company not having a share capital, the right may be exercised by members having not less than one tenth of the voting rights. They may write to the directors at the registered office requiring them to convene a meeting. This may be done by means of a single document signed by the necessary number of members, or it may be done by means of several documents making substantially the same requisition. The power for members to requisition a meeting may not be overridden by the articles.

The directors must convene a meeting within 21 days of receipt of the necessary requisitions and the date of the convened meeting must be not more than 28 days after it is convened. The directors are required to do this, but if they do not do so the members who requisitioned the meeting (or holders of shares representing half of them) may convene the meeting themselves.

A resigning auditor has the power to requisition an extraordinary general meeting.

Period of notice and entitlement to receive notice

The required length of notice is governed by Section 369 of the Act. The periods are:

- 21 days for an Annual General Meeting.

- 14 days for other general meetings of a limited company.

- Seven days for other general meetings of an unlimited company.

- 21 days for a meeting to pass a special resolution requiring a 75 per cent majority, a meeting to pass an ordinary resolution of which special notice has been given, or a meeting to pass an elective resolution requiring everyone to attend and approve it (in person or by proxy).

Notice must be given in writing or, subject to safeguards, by means of electronic communication. Section 369 provides that, subject to safeguards, notice may be given by means of electronic communication notwithstanding anything to the contrary in a company's articles. Electronic communication is explained in more detail in the next section of this chapter.

The period of notice must be clear days, excluding the date on which notice is served. In England and Wales the date of the meeting is also excluded, but this is not the case in Scotland. In the case of a dispute, notice will be deemed to have been received 48 hours after postage of a correctly stamped and addressed envelope.

Company articles may amend the above to a limited extent and in particular they may reduce (or extend) the 48 hour period. Company articles may provide for longer than the above periods of 21 days, 14 days or seven days, but they may not provide for shorter periods.

It is possible to hold a valid meeting without the above minimum periods of notice having been given. This is known as 'short notice' and the following criteria must be satisfied:

- In the case of an Annual General Meeting, consent must be given by everyone entitled to attend and vote.

- In the case of an Extraordinary General Meeting, consent must normally be given by persons representing at least 95 per cent of the shares carrying the right to attend and vote. This proportion is reduced to 90 per cent in the case of a private company which passes an elective resolution. Furthermore, consent must be given by a majority in number of those entitled to attend and vote.

The practical effect of the short notice criteria relating to an Extraordinary General Meeting may be illustrated with an example. If there are three shareholders and one holds 98 per cent of the shares, he cannot authorise short notice unless he has the support of at least one of the others.

It is not essential that consent to short notice be in writing, but it is good practice and avoids the possibility of disputes. Short notice means short notice; not no notice. Some notice must always be given.

Entitlement to receive notice is governed by the articles. However, a company's auditors must receive notice and this requirement may not be removed by the articles. It is normal for the articles to require notice to be sent to every member except for those with a registered address outside the United Kingdom, unless a United Kingdom address for the receipt of notices has been supplied.

Care should be taken if the company has shares that do not normally carry voting rights. Holders of such shares are normally entitled to receive notice if events have happened that entitle them to cast votes, such as the missing of a dividend.

Table A provides that all directors must receive notice of general meetings. Reg. 39 of Table A gives protection in the event of accidental omission to give proper notice, but it must of course be accidental. Reg. 39 reads:

> *'The accidental omission to give notice of a meeting to, or the non-receipt of notice of a meeting by, any person entitled to receive notice shall not invalidate the proceedings at that meeting'.*

Notice sent by means of electronic communication

This was made possible by the Companies Act 1985 (Electronic Communications) Order 2000 which came into force on 22nd December 2000. Electronic communication, subject to conditions, is permitted, notwithstanding anything to the contrary in a company's articles. Of course companies are permitted to use electronic communication. They are not compelled to do so.

There are two different methods but both may only be used to communicate with members who have agreed to accept communication in this way. Every member has the right to choose written communication.

The first method is to communicate directly with a member who has agreed to accept service in this manner and who has provided an 'address' for this purpose. The second method is to publish the notice on a website. This is only notification to members who have agreed to accept notice in this way.

Electronic communication is a big subject and it is not possible to cover all aspects here. Further reading may be essential if this method is to be used.

Details and contents of notice

The notice should state:

- The place of the meeting.

- The date and time of the meeting.

- A statement concerning the rights of members to appoint a proxy or proxies to attend and vote on their behalf.

- Whether the meeting is an Annual General Meeting or an Extraordinary General Meeting.

- A general description of each item of business to be conducted. This is additional to the precise wording of resolutions that are required in some cases.

- In the case of a special, extraordinary or elective resolution, the precise wording must be included.

The time, place and location of the meeting should be reasonably convenient for the members. So 2am on Lundy Island is not likely to be permitted.

The notice should be signed on behalf of the body calling the meeting as, for example 'by order of the board of directors .... secretary'.

Proxies

In the case of a company having a share capital, each member has the right to appoint a proxy to represent him at a general meeting of the company. Furthermore the appointed proxy need not be a member of the company. These rights are conferred by the Act and may not be removed by the company articles. However, the articles may give additional rights and may be important when considering points of detail.

The Act does not confer these rights on members of a company limited by guarantee, and rights (if any) are those conferred by the articles. If Table C applies unamended, members have the same rights as given by Table A to the members of a company limited by shares. The following is the position if Table A applies unamended.

A proxy does count when establishing whether or not a quorum is present. In a private company the proxy has the same right to speak as the member that he represents. In a public company the proxy does not have the right to speak and may only do so with the permission of the chairman. In both public and private companies a proxy may not vote on a show of hands but may join in a demand for a poll and may vote in a poll.

It is not a requirement that a suitable proxy form be sent out with notices, though it is usually done. It is permitted for members to prepare their own form. If a form is sent with the notices, the same form must be sent to all members entitled to vote. It is most definitely not permitted to send proxy forms only to members considered likely to vote in a certain way. However, it is permissible to send proxy forms only to members who request them.

There are two types of proxy form. One appoints a person as proxy and gives no voting instructions. This is known as the 'open form'. The other appoints a person as proxy and gives specific voting instructions on the various resolutions. Examples of suitable formats are given in Regs. 60 and 61 of Table A. These forms are for guidance and the directors are not compelled to follow the wording exactly. Listed companies are required to use a form of proxy that enables the member to give voting instructions. Although any person may be appointed a proxy, in practice most appointments are of directors.

Quorum

The rules concerning a quorum depend on the articles. Unless the articles provide differently, a quorum is two members present in person. The definition of 'present in person' includes proxies and it also includes company representatives.

The articles should also provide what happens if a quorum is not present. Table A provides as follows:

- If a quorum is not present within 30 minutes of the time appointed for the start of the meeting, then the meeting is adjourned to the same place, at the same day and time the following week. However, the directors may decide to vary this.

- The meeting must be adjourned if, even though a quorum was present at the start of the meeting, attendance drops during the meeting to a figure below that for a quorum.

If a company has fewer members than the number fixed for a quorum by the articles, a valid meeting may be held if all members are present by person or by proxy. This is the case in a single-member company.

Adjournment

The articles may determine precise powers and procedures concerning adjournment of meetings. A meeting must be adjourned if a quorum is not present and this was explained in detail above.

Normally, the decision to adjourn a meeting must be taken by the meeting itself. Only in exceptional circumstances does the decision rest with the chairman. Reg. 45 of Table A states that the chairman may adjourn with the consent of the meeting, and must adjourn if so directed by the meeting. It goes on to say that no business shall be transacted at an adjourned meeting that could not have been transacted at the original meeting. If the adjournment is for 14 days or more, seven clear days notice of time, place and the general nature of the business must be given.

The chairman has authority to adjourn the meeting without the consent of the members if serious misconduct prevents the meeting being properly held. This right cannot be removed by company articles. He may also adjourn to assist the business of the meeting. In both cases the adjournment may only be for as long as is necessary.

The chairman

The question of who is to act as chairman of a general meeting is resolved according to the articles. Table A provides that, if he is present and willing to act, it will be the chairman of the Board. If this is not the case it will be one of the other directors. If, after 15 minutes from the nominated time of the start of the meeting no director is present and willing to act, the voting members present may elect one of their number to the position.

The powers and duties of the chairman will, to some extent, depend on the articles. The chairman must (in order of priority) act in a way that satisfies the law, company articles and natural fairness and efficiency. Table A gives the chairman a casting vote which may be exercised in addition to any other vote that he may have, but it is possible for company articles to exclude a casting vote.

As well as any requirements stipulated by the articles, the chairman has common law duties to put the resolutions to the meeting, permit fair and reasonable discussion, supervise lawful, fair and efficient voting and announce the results of the voting.

Voting

Voting must be in accordance with company articles and, as with other issues, Table A will apply so long as it is not inconsistent with company articles. Unless articles stipulate otherwise, which is not usually the case, an initial vote is taken on a show of hands. In the case of a company limited by guarantee it is one member one vote and the result of this vote decides the issue.

Unless articles provide otherwise, which is not usually the case, each member present may only cast one vote. This is regardless of the number of shares held and regardless of the number of members for which he is acting as proxy. This sounds very unfair but the remedy lies in the ability to demand a poll. Table A does not allow proxy votes to be cast on a show of hands, but again the remedy lies in the ability to demand a poll. A representative of a corporate shareholder may vote on a show of hands.

The chairman will announce the result of the vote on a show of hands. He may do this by stating the number for or against, or he may do so by stating that one side or the other is in the majority. If a resolution has been passed as a special, extraordinary or elective resolution, the chairman should state that this is the case. Unless a poll is demanded, the chairman's decision of the vote, duly minuted, is conclusive. However, it may be challenged later in the case of fraud or if there has been an obvious mistake.

Under Table A, the chairman may demand a poll following the result of a vote on a show of hands. In practice he may do this for any reason, including the fact that the result was not what he hoped it would be. Other reasons may include a realisation that the result is not absolutely clear, and a belief that a poll may well produce a different result. The chairman may be said in these circumstances to have a duty to call for a poll.

Members may also demand a poll. Section 373(1) of the Act makes it impossible for company articles to exclude this right, other than on a vote for the election of the chairman of the meeting or the adjournment of the meeting. The same section provides that a poll must be held if it is demanded by any of:

- not less than five members entitled to vote at the meeting

- a member or members representing not less than one tenth of the total voting rights of all the members having the right to vote at the meeting

- a member or members holding not less than one tenth of the total paid up capital of the company.

This right too cannot be removed by company articles, although company articles may allow a poll to be demanded by lower proportions. A proxy does count for the purpose of demanding a poll.

In a poll it is normal for one vote to attach to each voting share, though to a limited extent company articles may vary this. Depending on circumstances, a poll may be easy to conduct or it may be very complicated. A poll should be held as soon as possible and is usually held at once. However, depending on circumstances, it may be held later at the same meeting, at an adjourned meeting or by post. A poll held later remains part of the proceedings of the meeting.

Minutes

Both the Act and Table A (in reg. 100) require that minutes be taken and kept, but neither says much about what must be included and the procedures that must be followed. Section 382(1) of the Act states:

> 'Every company shall cause minutes of all proceedings of general meetings, all proceedings at meetings of its directors and where there are managers, all proceedings at meetings of its managers to be entered in books kept for that propose.'

It is permitted for details of attendance to be recorded in a separate attendance register, and it is permitted for the minutes to be kept in a loose-leaf system rather than in a bound book. The style of the minutes may vary according to the wishes of the people concerned. It is acceptable, and many people consider desirable, for the minutes to record just the decisions made and the key facts, such as adjournments etc. If a resolution is passed as a special, extraordinary or elective resolution, this should be recorded by the minutes.

Neither the Act nor Table A set out a procedure for approval of the minutes, though it is possible that individual articles may do so. Procedure is therefore a matter of good practice and the wishes of the members and directors.

It is usually wise to prepare the minutes as soon as possible after the meeting and to show them to the chairman so that they may be checked with his recollection and notes (if any). The minutes should then be circulated as soon as possible to all directors. At the next board meeting the chairman should ask if the minutes of the general meeting are approved and then, if the answer is affirmative, should sign them. Hopefully this should not take more than a few seconds.

This is done in many companies but it is considered 'good practice' and is not a legal requirement. Other practices may be allowed and followed. Members, directors and auditors have the right of access to the minutes of members' meetings.

Electronic general meetings

An electronic general meeting is one held by means of the telephone or audio-visual links. The position is not absolutely clear but it is generally accepted that such meetings are not permitted, notwithstanding anything to the contrary in the articles. A company general meeting necessitates all participants meeting at one place, though subject to safeguards, electronic links within one building may be allowed.

Checklist

- There are four standard items of business for an Annual General Meeting. They are listed in the early part of this chapter.

- An Annual General Meeting must be held within 15 months of the last Annual General Meeting. Furthermore, an Annual General Meeting must be held in each calendar year.

- Under the elective regime, a private company may, subject to safeguards and unanimous consent, elect to dispense with Annual General Meetings.

- An Extraordinary General Meeting is any general meeting that is not an Annual General Meeting. The purpose of an Extraordinary General meeting is to conduct special business.

- Different types of resolution and notice are required for different items of business. Details are in this chapter.

- Extraordinary resolutions and special resolutions both need a 75 per cent majority.

- Written resolutions avoid the need to hold a meeting. 100 per cent support is needed and they are only available to private companies.

- The elective regime gives private companies a chance to cut down on meetings. 100 per cent support is needed.

- It is normal for the directors to convene both Annual General Meetings and Extraordinary General Meetings. However, it is possible for members to requisition a meeting, which must then be held.

- It is important that notice of meetings is given to all people entitled to receive notice.

- It is important that the correct periods of notice are given.

- It is important that correct notice of business and wording of resolutions is given.

- In the case of a company having a share capital a notice convening a meeting, or a document accompanying the notice, must include a statement concerning the rights of members to appoint a proxy or proxies.

- A proxy may not vote on a show of hands, but may demand a poll and vote in a poll.

- Unless company articles provide differently, a quorum is two members present in person or by proxy.

- Meetings may be adjourned, and in some circumstances must be adjourned.

- Voting must be in accordance with the articles.

- Unless articles provide differently, an initial vote is on a show of hands based on one vote for each member present.

- In the case of a company having a share capital the chairman or members may call for a poll. A poll usually gives one vote to each share.

- In the case of a company limited by guarantee it is one member one vote.

- Subject to safeguards, notice of meetings may be given electronically. All members have the right to insist on written notice.

- Electronic general meetings are not permitted.

- It is a legal requirement that minutes be taken and kept. There is quite a bit of freedom to decide 'good practice'.

chapter twelve

Board meetings

Introduction

The articles and Table A

The calling of Board Meetings and due notice

Quorum

Directors' interests

The chairman

A deficiency in the number of directors

Written resolutions of directors

Minutes

Committees and other meetings

Electronic board meetings

Checklist

Introduction

The directors are responsible for the management of a company and meetings are therefore of great importance. Board Meetings play a significant part in a list of the company secretary's duties and a close working relationship with the chairman is important. The company secretary should:

- Call Board Meetings and make arrangements for them.

- Contribute to the efficient running of them.

- Give advice when he is asked by the chairman or other directors, and sometimes give advice when he is not asked.

- Produce the minutes and keep the other records.

The articles and Table A

Directors are mostly free to set their own rules for Board Meetings and to conduct them as they see fit. This is said with the big proviso that they must pay due regard to the articles of the company. Company articles generally contain detailed provisions concerning Board Meetings and Table A does so. Table A applies unless it is inconsistent with specific articles.

Appendix A reproduces Table A in full. Regs. 88 to 98 concern the 'Proceedings of Directors'. Some of the key points of Table A are as follows:

- Subject to the articles, the directors may regulate their proceedings as they see fit (reg. 88).

- Any director may call a meeting of directors (reg. 88).

- The secretary must call a meeting of directors if requested to do so by any director (reg. 88).

- Matters at a meeting will be settled by a majority of votes (reg. 88).

- The chairman has a second or casting vote (reg. 88).

- The number of a quorum may be fixed by the directors, but in the absence of a decision it is two (reg. 89).

- The directors may appoint one of their number as chairman and may remove him from that position (reg. 91).

- A unanimously approved written resolution is valid (reg. 93).

- A director must not vote on a matter in which he has a material interest. There are specified exceptions (reg. 94).

It is the first sentence of reg. 88 which states that, subject to the articles, the directors may regulate their proceedings as they see fit. Company secretaries should note the phrase 'subject to the provisions of the articles'. It is very important that due regard is paid to the articles, whether or not Table A applies.

Reg. 84 of Table A includes:

> *'Subject to the provisions of the Act, the directors may appoint one or more of their number to the office of managing director or to any other executive office under the company.'*

The calling of Board Meetings and due notice

Practices vary enormously. Almost all public companies and large private companies hold regular meetings, perhaps monthly, and with dates fixed many months in advance. This is particularly important when there are non-executive directors and executive directors who travel a lot. At the other extreme, in a small private company Board Meetings can consist of a conversation in a corridor. Such a practice is undesirable and in many circumstances may not constitute a valid meeting, but readers will know that, regardless of theory, it does happen.

In most cases a meeting is not valid unless all directors have knowledge of it and have a chance to attend. This is so, even if a board consists of 20 directors and 19 attend and vote unanimously in favour of a particular resolution. All directors must have a reasonable opportunity of attending and expressing a point of view. However, Table A (reg. 88) states that it is not necessary to give notice to a director who is out of the United Kingdom. This must be interpreted in a reasonable way. Directors are not permitted to call a meeting immediately a fellow director's plane clears territorial waters and with the intention of frustrating his ability to attend.

There is no specific requirement that notice of a Board Meeting should be given and in an emergency it may be necessary to hold a meeting without notice. Nevertheless, it is desirable and good practice to give reasonable notice, and in most cases it is good practice to give long notice. This is fair to all directors and overcomes any possibility of the proceedings being invalid on these grounds. It is also good practice because directors have a chance to make effective preparations.

Under Table A (reg. 88) any director may call a Board Meeting, and the company secretary must do so if requested by any director. This is a safeguard for all concerned, but normal good practice is for the chairman to call meetings after consulting fellow directors and the company secretary. It is also good practice for the company secretary to notify all directors in writing of the date, time and place. At the same time or later the company secretary should notify the directors in writing of the details of the agenda and circulate papers for the meeting. Unless it is prohibited by the articles, notice may be given orally, but this is not good practice and company secretaries should give notice in writing.

Quorum

The articles may fix the quorum for Board Meetings. Table A gives the directors the power to fix the quorum, but states that if they do not do so it shall be two directors.

A director who is not allowed to vote on a particular item of business is not counted when establishing whether or not a quorum is present. This can happen, for example, if a vote is taken on a matter in which a director has a material interest.

Directors' interests

It is usually the case that a director is not permitted to vote at a Board Meeting on a matter in which he has a material interest. This is the position under Table A (reg. 94), but reg. 94 makes an exception in limited, specified circumstances. Reg. 96 permits the company, by ordinary resolution in a general meeting, to extend these circumstances.

A director must disclose to the board any material interest that he has in a contract that is before the board. This obligation is additional to, and separate from, the obligation not to vote on such a contract. This obligation is imposed by Section 317 of the Act, not by Table A.

The chairman

Table A (reg. 91) states that the directors may appoint a chairman and may remove him from that office. In practice, although it is not usually a requirement, there are overwhelming advantages in having a chairman and one is almost always elected. Some company articles specify that the position of chairman will be filled.

Reg. 88 of Table A gives the chairman a second or casting vote and this power is obviously very significant. It should also be noted that reg. 98 of Table A allows the chairman to rule on the right of a director to vote, but that he may not rule on his own right to vote.

The chairman has a particular responsibility for calling board meetings and for seeing that they are conducted efficiently and fairly. The relationship between the company secretary and the chairman is very important and the chairman may need to rely on the company secretary's support and advice. Hopefully the relationship is one of mutual trust and respect. Whether or not this is the case, there may be times when the company secretary needs to express an opinion to the chairman very clearly and unambiguously. The company secretary should not sit quietly if rules are disregarded and it is possible that he will at times need to give clear and unambiguous advice to the directors and not just to the chairman.

The chairman will have a dual responsibility. On the one hand he is a director of the board and is entitled to pursue his own point of view. On the other hand he has a duty to allow all opinions to be expressed fairly, even when they are in conflict with his own.

Many chairman try to guide the board to a unanimous decision or a consensus agreement, and try to achieve this with very few formal votes. Many British prime ministers are said to run their cabinets in this way, though they have the advantage of being able to dismiss their cabinet colleagues. Other chairmen rely more on formal votes. Neither style is right or wrong, but the company must always act in accordance with company law and the articles. Unanimity or consensus should only be recorded if the directors genuinely wish, or are willing to accept, unanimity or consensus.

A deficiency in the number of directors

A problem will arise if the number of directors falls below the number required for a quorum. Reference should be made to the articles and it should be noted that reg. 90 of Table A states '... *the continuing directors or director may act only for the purpose of filling vacancies or calling a general meeting*'. Such a general meeting can of course be for the purpose of appointing additional directors. Table A provides that the directors can fill casual vacancies or appoint additional directors up to any maximum number fixed by the articles.

If there are no directors left, the members may convene a meeting to appoint directors.

Written resolutions of directors

Provision for this is made by reg. 93 of Table A. If this applies, it operates in a similar way to the facility available to members and described in Chapter 12. To be effective, signatures must be obtained from 100 per cent of directors entitled to receive notice of a meeting. Written resolutions are very useful and are widely used.

Minutes

Both the Act and Table A require that minutes be taken and kept, but neither says much about what must be included and the procedures that must be followed. Section 382(1) of the Act states:

> *'Every company shall cause minutes of all proceedings of general meetings, all proceedings at meetings of its directors and where there are managers, all proceedings at meetings of its managers to be entered in books kept for that purpose.'*

Table A requires the minutes to include details of all appointments of officers made by the directors and the names of the directors present. It is permitted for details of attendance to be recorded in a separate attendance register.

The style of the minutes may vary according to the inclinations of the directors and of the company secretary. In most circumstances it is sufficient to list the items of business and the decisions taken. It is usual to follow this pattern and not record the ebb and flow of the discussions and the points of view expressed. However, fuller minutes may be made if it is the wish of the people concerned. Certain things should be minuted in addition to the decisions made. Examples are the identity of the chairman and a statement by a director that he has a material interest in a matter under consideration.

Fuller minutes should be considered if there is serious and fundamental disagreement, bad feeling or confusion. A director's request that his dissent be minuted should be accommodated. Fuller minutes should also be considered if the company faces financial difficulties. In these circumstances it may be important that directors are able to show the reasons for the decisions made.

Neither the Act nor Table A sets out a procedure for approval of the minutes, though it is possible that individual articles may do so. Procedure, therefore, is a matter of good practice and the wishes of the directors.

It is usually wise to prepare the minutes as soon as possible after the meeting and to show them to the chairman so that they can be checked with his recollection and notes (if any). The minutes should then be circulated as soon as possible to all directors. At the next board meeting the chairman should ask if the minutes are approved and then, if the answer is affirmative, should sign them. Hopefully this should not take more than a few seconds.

This is done in many companies, but it is considered 'good practice' and is not a legal requirement. Other practices may be allowed and followed. Directors and auditors have access to board minutes but members may only have access with the permission of the directors. It is therefore a good idea to keep board minutes separate from the minutes of general meetings.

Committees and other meetings

Some readers will study this chapter and then say 'That's all very well, but it's not the way it happens in my company.' It should indeed be recognised that in some companies theory and practice do diverge widely. There are probably dangers, especially if there is a dominant director and even more so if he is also a major shareholder, but nothing too terrible may happen as a result. The company secretary and all the directors should know the law, so that what happens occurs with their informed consent. Nevertheless, there may be dangers and that fact should not be overlooked. This chapter aims to show the lawful way of doing things and also to illustrate good practice.

It should also be said that there may be misunderstandings about different types of meetings of directors. There are four types as follows:

- A full, formal Board Meeting.

- A formal meeting of a committee of directors.

- Another type of meeting of directors.

- An 'ad hoc' gathering of two or more directors.

This chapter concerns full, formal Board Meetings and meetings of board committees. Meetings of two or more directors do not necessarily constitute Board Meetings or meetings of a Board committee. They may be meeting in a managerial or other capacity and these meetings are the last two headings on the above list. Meetings of the Board, or of a Board committee, are appropriate for legal and constitutional matters and also for strategic planning and very important operational decisions. Such meetings may also be used for more routine management matters but management meetings may be considered more appropriate.

Reg. 72 of Table A states the '*directors may delegate any of their powers to any committee consisting of one or more directors. They may also delegate to any managing director or any director holding any other executive office such of their powers as they consider desirable to be exercised by him*'. The setting up of Board committees is common practice. Audit committees and remuneration committees are frequently-encountered examples, as are committees to handle sealings and share transfers.

It is good practice for the membership of a Board committee to be approved and minuted by the full Board. The same applies to its terms of reference and any directions as to its chairman, operation, etc. The full Board may set up a committee and the full Board can, of course, terminate a committee at any time.

Electronic board meetings

An electronic board meeting is one held by means of the telephone or audio-visual links. Such meetings are relatively common and can be very useful.

Reg.88 of Table A states *that 'Subject to the provisions of the articles, the directors may regulate their proceedings as they see fit.'* Various implications have not been fully tested but it is considered that in most circumstances this allows telephone board meetings. Some companies put the matter entirely beyond doubt with specially adapted articles and this is recommended. Of course the normal rules about directors being informed of the meeting and having the right to attend still apply.

It is essential that all directors be able to hear each other and speak to each other at all times. This means that if there are more than two directors, a conference call must be set up. It is not acceptable for the chairman to talk to some directors, then report the conversation to other directors.

Checklist

- Due regard must be paid to company articles. Table A has quite a lot to say and will apply unless it is inconsistent with other articles.

- Directors are mostly free to set their own rules for Board Meetings and to conduct them as they see fit. Table A provides for this.

- Under Table A, the company secretary must call a Board Meeting if requested to do so by any director.

- Under Table A, the chairman has a second or casting vote.

- Under Table A, a unanimous written resolution is valid.

- In most cases a meeting is not valid unless all directors knew of it and had a chance to attend.

- It is good practice to give all directors, in writing, as much notice as possible of meetings, including place, date and time. However, a valid meeting may be called at short notice.

- Under Table A, directors may fix the quorum, but if they do not do so it is two.

- Telephone board meetings are, in many cases and subject to safeguards, permitted. They are relatively common and can be very useful.

- A director must disclose a material interest to a Board Meeting and generally may not vote on the matter. There are exceptions.

- Under Table A, the directors appoint the chairman and may remove him.

- The company secretary should speak up very clearly if rules are disregarded or he is worried about procedure. He should do this even if his views are not sought.

- The company secretary should keep the attendance record and the minutes. In most cases, but not all, it is sufficient simply to record decisions made.

- The Act and good practice are not followed in some companies. This may be dangerous and the company secretary should say so.

- Under Table A, directors may delegate any of their powers to a committee of directors. A committee may consist of one or more directors.

chapter thirteen

Transfer and transmission of shares

Introduction

Transfer of shares

CREST in outline

Forged transfers

Bearer shares

Transmission of shares

Share certificates

Stamp duty

Form J30: Stock transfer

Checklist

Introduction

One of the features of the Anglo-Saxon joint stock company is that membership may be transferred or transmitted. Transfer happens at the wish of the member (transferor), whereas transmission happens due to the incapacity (including death) of the member. Some companies, by their articles, restrict the right to transfer shares, but marketability and ease of transfer are key attractions of our system.

Efficient transfer, as provided by law and company articles, is very important for a company and its members. Achievement of this is an important responsibility of the company secretary. There may be unfortunate consequences if mistakes are made.

This chapter relates exclusively to the 96 per cent of British companies that have a share capital. This is because membership of a company limited by guarantee cannot be transferred and terminates upon death. Such a company may create new members in accordance with the terms of its constitution.

Transfer of shares

Ownership of shares is freely transferable, subject to any restrictions that may be contained in a company's articles. In practice, many private companies do have restrictions and these often give the directors the right to refuse to register a transfer. Whether or not the articles do restrict the transfer of shares, a company cannot be compelled to register a transfer to a minor.

A company is only permitted to register a transfer of shares if a properly completed instrument of transfer is delivered to it. This is a requirement of section 183(1) of the Act and company articles cannot override it. Transfer of listed shares is normally done under the CREST system which is explained in outline later in this chapter. Otherwise transfer must be by means of an approved Stock Transfer Form. A completed example is given just before the Checklist at the end of this chapter.

The necessary steps are as follows:

- The person owning the shares will complete and execute the instrument of transfer and give it to the purchaser, together with the corresponding share certificate.

- The purchaser is liable to pay the consideration to the seller.

- The purchaser will pay the stamp duty. There is a separate section of this chapter on stamp duty.

- The purchaser will deliver the stamped instrument of transfer, together with the share certificate, to the company.

- The company secretary will check that everything is in order. If this is the case, the transfer will be considered by the directors or in accordance with a procedure approved by the directors.

- When the directors have approved the transfer, the register of members will be amended and a new share certificate will be issued to the purchaser. This should be done within two months of the Share Transfer Form being lodged. The old certificate must be cancelled and the documents filed.

The above does, of course, assume the sale of the shares and it also assumes that all the shares represented by a particular certificate are sold. If only some shares are sold, the company will issue two new certificates. One of these is to the purchaser, and one is to the seller for the number of shares that he still holds.

CREST in outline

CREST is a system for the dematerialised holding and transfer of securities. It is operated by CRESTCO Ltd, a company that is owned by a range of interested parties. It is for listed companies and although it is not compulsory, the great majority of transfers in listed companies are accomplished by means of the CREST system.

Where a company's shares have been admitted to CREST, the register of members will include uncertificated accounts for CREST members. Movements between these accounts are accomplished without the use of paper transfers and are authorised by electronic messages from the system operator. There is daily reconciliation between the operator and the registrar and by the operator with members of the system.

The CREST system entails shares being held in nominee names and some people believe that this has unfortunate consequences in distancing individual shareholders from the companies in which they invest. In the CREST system only the total of a nominee company's holding will be shown in the register of a company. One dividend payment will be made to the nominee company, which will in turn pay or credit individual accounts. Transfers of shares within the CREST system are made electronically, permitting economies and swifter execution.

Forged transfers

A forged transfer cannot deprive the true, registered member of his rights in the company. He is entitled to the return of the shares or equivalent shares, and retains rights to dividends and other benefits attaching to the shares. In the case of a forged transfer, the transferee does not acquire rights in the shares, even if he has acted in good faith. Even the receipt of a share certificate from the company does not alter this.

It does not follow that a company will have no liability at all. It may do so if it accepts the transfer and issues a share certificate. A problem may arise if this share certificate is used in a further transfer and another party acquires the shares in good faith for value. In these circumstances the company will be stopped from denying the share certificate that it has issued. It is common practice for companies to take out insurance against losses that may occur in this way.

Bearer shares

Bearer shares (or warrants) are not common in this country but they may be encountered. They are more common in some other countries and are sometimes issued by British companies to suit shareholders in these countries. A company may issue bearer warrants for fully paid shares if authorised to do so by its articles.

A bearer share warrant is a negotiable instrument and title passes by mere delivery. This means that a person acting in good faith may acquire a good title, even if the title of the person passing the warrant is defective. There are obvious difficulties concerning stamp duty as the change of ownership is not registered when a warrant is passed. For this reason no duty is levied at this stage. However, duty of triple the duty payable at market value is levied when the warrant is first issued. It is the practice for bearer warrants to have coupons attached. A coupon is submitted to the company each time that a dividend payment is claimed.

The company secretary should keep a register detailing bearer warrants issued. If the articles permit, bearer warrants may be surrendered for registered shares.

Transmission of shares

Transfer of shares takes place as a result of a decision by a member to sell or give away his shares. A duly signed and stamped instrument of transfer must be delivered to the company. Transmission of shares entails a change in the registered owner as a result of one of the following circumstances:

- Death of a member.

- Bankruptcy of a member.

- A member becomes of unsound mind.

In the event of one of these sad occurrences, the company must deal with, respectively:

- The personal representatives of the deceased member. These may be executors or administrators.

- The trustee in bankruptcy.

- The committee or receiver of the member.

It will be readily appreciated that there are dangers for the company in these situations. Care must be taken to ensure that dealings only take place with people who have the necessary authority. To this end it is essential that the correct documentation is obtained and inspected.

Following the death of a member, the necessary procedure and the precise obligations of the company will depend on the articles. Regs. 29 to 31 of Table A deal with transmission of shares. The company's obligations are to the personal representatives of a deceased member, not to the beneficiaries of his estate. Reg. 30 gives a personal representative the right to be registered as a member, but a company's articles may give the directors the right to refuse a transfer. In practice it is usually desirable to have the personal representatives entered as members unless the estate is dealt with swiftly. Similar provisions apply in cases of bankruptcy and of members becoming of unsound mind.

The following steps are necessary in connection with the transmission of shares:

- The company secretary should obtain the correct documentation and check it thoroughly. This will vary according to circumstances and it should be noted that Scottish law differs from the law in England and Wales. The relevant share certificate should also be submitted.

- The company secretary should endorse the fact of the documentation upon appropriate company records.

- If a representative wishes the shares to be transferred into his own name, a letter requesting this should be sent to the company. Alternatively, the representative may transfer the shares. This may be done, for example, when the shares have been willed to a specified beneficiary.

If shares are held in joint names, the death of one holder results in the title passing to the surviving joint holder or holders. It is of course necessary for proof of death to be provided to the company.

If the circumstances are not straightforward or if the company secretary has doubts about his competence in this area, it may be wise for him to seek legal advice. This may be particularly appropriate if a member is, or may be, bankrupt or of unsound mind.

Share certificates

A genuine share certificate issued in accordance with a company's articles is prima facie evidence of the title to the shares of the person named. The company is estopped from denying that entitlement. Furthermore, if such a share certificate describes shares as fully paid, then this is prima facie evidence that the shares are fully paid. It will therefore be readily appreciated that a share certificate is an important document and that considerable care must be exercised.

Most company articles provide that a share certificate must be signed by two directors, or by one director and the company secretary. When large numbers of certificates are required, company articles sometimes provide that signatures are not necessary. A share certificate must be executed by the company. This used to mean that it had to bear the company seal, but this is no longer essential.

There are no statutory requirements relating to the size, layout, etc of share certificates, but common sense and good practice indicate the following:

- The full, correct name should be stated.

- The company's registered number should be stated.

- The class of share should be stated.

- The denomination should be stated.

- The full name of the shareholder should be stated.

- The certificate should state that the shares are fully paid if this is the case. If the shares are partly paid, the amount paid should be stated.

- The serial number of the certificate should be stated.

- The certificate should be signed and executed. The date of issue should be stated.

A share certificate must, subject to the articles, be ready for issue within two months of allotment or two months of lodgement of the transfer document. The terms of an issue of shares may vary this two month period. This is not a statutory requirement, but it is understood to be a common law obligation.

The issue of replacement certificates depends on the articles. Reg. 7 of Table A provides as follows:

'If a share certificate is defaced, worn-out, lost or destroyed, it may be renewed on such terms (if any) as to evidence and indemnity and payment of the expenses reasonably incurred by the company in investigating evidence as the directors may determine but otherwise free of charge, and (in the case of defacement or wearing-out) on delivery up of the old certificate.'

If the old certificate is still in existence it should be surrendered before a replacement is issued. Companies, particularly listed companies, frequently secure a suitable indemnity before issuing a replacement certificate. This safeguard is recommended in most situations.

Stamp duty

A company is not permitted to register a transfer that has not been properly stamped. This is important and the company secretary may incur personal penalties if it is disregarded.

Stamping is the responsibility of the transferee and it must be done before the form is submitted to the company. At the time of publication stamp duty is 50p per £100, or part of £100, of the consideration. This means, for example, that £5.00 stamp duty is payable if the consideration is £940.

In certain cases stamp duty is not payable and these are listed on the rear side of stock transfer forms. If one of these circumstances applies, the certificate on the rear of a stock transfer form must be completed.

The procedure is for the stock transfer form to be submitted to a Stamp Office of the Inland Revenue, together with payment for the appropriate amount of duty. If all is in order, the Inland Revenue Stamp Office will impress the form to mark that duty has been paid. The Inland Revenue Stamp Offices are located as follows:

Belfast Stamp Office
Ground Floor
Dorchester House
52-58 Great Victoria Street
Belfast BT2 7QJ
Tel: 02890 505314

Birmingham Stamp Office
5th Floor
Norfolk House Royal
Smallbrook Queensway
Birmingham B5 4LA
Tel: 0121 633 3313

Bristol Stamp Office
First Floor
The Pithay
All Saints Street
Bristol BS1 2NY
Tel: 0117 927 2022

Edinburgh Stamp Office
Garfield House
5 Bankhead Avenue
Edinburgh EH11 4BF
Tel: 0131 442 3161

London Stamp Office
Personal Callers only:
South West Wing
Bush House
Strand
London WC2B 4QN
Tel: 020 7438 7452

Manchester Office
Upper 5th Floor
Royal Exchange
Exchange Street
Manchester M2 7EB
Tel: 0161 834 8020

Newcastle Stamp Office
4th Floor
Weardale House
District 1
Washington
Tyne and Wear NE37 1LW
Tel: 0191 201 7413

Worthing Stamp Office
Postal applications only
Ground Floor
East Block
Barrington Road
Worthing
West Sussex BN12 4XJ
Tel: 01903 508930

STOCK TRANSFER FORM J30

STOCK TRANSFER FORM		
J30	(Above this line for Registrars only)	

Certificate lodged with the Registrar

Consideration Money £10,000.00 . . . . .

(For completion by the Registrar/Stock Exchange)

Full name of Undertaking.	J. R. Blognalt Limited
Full description of Security.	Ordinary shares of 20p each

Number or amount of Shares, Stock or other security and, in figures column only, number and denomination of units, if any	Words Ten thousand	Figures 10,000 (units of)

Name(s) of registered holder(s) should be given in full: the address should be given where there is only one holder.

If the transfer is not made by the registered holder(s) insert also the name(s) and capacity (e.g., Executor(s)) of the person(s) making the transfer.

In the name(s) of

Peter Graham Smith
49 Station Street
Tring
Hertfordshire
HP16 9LU

. . . .
Account Designation (if any)

. . . .

I/We hereby transfer the above security out of the name(s) aforesaid to the person(s) named below *or to the several persons named in Parts 2 of Brokers Transfer Forms relating to the above security.*

Delete words in italics except for stock exchange transactions.

Signature(s) of transferor(s)

1. *P. G. Smith*

2. . . . .

3. . . . .

4. . . . .

A body corporate should execute this transfer under its common seal or otherwise in accordance with applicable statutory requirements

Stamp of Selling Broker(s) or, for transactions which are not stock exchange transactions, of Agent(s), if any, acting for the Transferor(s).

Date . . . .

Full name(s) and full postal address(es) (including County or, if applicable, Postal District number) of the person(s) to whom the security is transferred.

Please state title, if any, or whether Mr., Mrs. or Miss.

Please complete in typewriting or in Block Capitals.

Mrs Louise Dorothy Jones
31 Elm Close
Aylesbury
Buckinghamshire
HP19 4DD

. . . .
Account Designation (if any)

. . . .

SPECIMEN

I/We request that such entries be made in the register as are necessary to give effect to this transfer.

Stamp of Buying Broker(s) (if any)	Stamp or name and address of person lodging this form (if other than the Buying Broker(s))

PLEASE SIGN HERE

Reference to the Registrar in this form means the registrar or registration agent of the undertaking, <u>not</u> the Registrar of Companies at Companies House

JSF0020 REV: 4.0 12.97

FORM of CERTIFICATE REQUIRED WHERE TRANSFER IS NOT LIABLE TO STAMP DUTY
Pursuant to the Stamp Duty (Exempt Instruments) Regulations 1987

(1) Delete as appropriate
(2) Insert "A", "B" or appropriate category

(1) I/We hereby certify that this instrument falls within category (2)_____ in the schedule to the Stamp Duty (Exempt Instruments) Regulations 1987, set out below.

*Signature(s)

*Description: "Transferor", "Solicitor", or state capacity of other person duly authorised to sign and giving the certificate from his known knowledge of the transaction.

Date _____ 19 _____

*NOTE - The above certificate should be signed by (i) the transferor(s) or (ii) a solicitor or other person (e.g. bank acting as trustee or executor) having a full knowledge of the facts. Such other person must state the capacity in which he signs, that he is authorised so to sign and gives the certificate from his own knowledge of the transaction.

SCHEDULE

A. The vesting of property subject to a trust in the trustees of the trust on the appointment of a new trustee, or in the continuing trustees on the retirement of a trustee.
B. The conveyance or transfer of property the subject of a specific devise or legacy to the beneficiary named in the will (or his nominee).
C. The conveyance or transfer of property which forms part of an intestate's estate to the person entitled on intestacy (or his nominee).
D. The appropriation of property within section 84(4) of the Finance Act 1985 (death: appropriation in satisfaction of a general legacy of money) or section 84(5) or (7) of that Act (death: appropriation in satisfaction of any interest of surviving spouse and in Scotland also of any interest of issue).
E. The conveyance or transfer of property which forms part of the residuary estate of a testator to a beneficiary (or his nominee) entitled solely by virtue of his entitlement under the will.
F. The conveyance or transfer of property out of a settlement in or towards satisfaction of a beneficiary's interest, not being an interest acquired for money or money's worth, being a conveyance or transfer constituting a distribution of property in accordance with the provisions of the settlement.
G. The conveyance or transfer of property on and in consideration only of marriage to a party to the marriage (or his nominee) or to trustees to be held on the terms of a settlement made in consideration only of the marriage.
H. The conveyance or transfer of property within section 83(1) of the Finance Act 1985 (transfers in connection with divorce etc.).
I. The conveyance or transfer by the liquidator of property which formed part of the assets of the company in liquidation to a shareholder of that company (or his nominee) in or towards satisfaction of the shareholder's rights on a winding-up.
J. The grant in fee simple of an easement in or over land for no consideration in money or money's worth.
K. The grant of a servitude for no consideration in money or money's worth.
L. The conveyance or transfer of property operating as a voluntary disposition *inter vivos* for no consideration in money or money's worth nor any consideration referred to in section 57 of the Stamp Act 1891 (conveyance in consideration of a debt etc.).
M. The conveyance or transfer of property by an instrument within section 84(1) of the Finance Act 1985 (death: varying disposition).

Instructional Notes
1. In order to obtain exemption from Stamp Duty on transactions described in the above schedule the Certificate must be completed and may then be lodged for registration or otherwise acted upon. Adjudication by the Stamp Office is not required.
2. This form does not apply to transactions falling within categories (a) and (b) in the form of certificate required where the transfer is not liable to ad valorem stamp duty set out below. In these cases the form of certificate printed below should be used. Transactions within either of those categories require submission of the form to the Stamp Office and remain liable to 50p duty.

FORM OF CERTIFICATE REQUIRED WHERE TRANSFER IS NOT LIABLE TO
AD VALOREM STAMP DUTY

Instruments of transfer are liable to a fixed duty of 50p when the transaction falls within one of the following categories:-

a Transfer by way of security for a loan or re-transfer to the original transferor on repayment of a loan.
b Transfer, not on a sale and not arising under any contract of sale and where no beneficial interest in the property passes: (i) to a person who is a mere nominee of, and is nominated only by, the transferor; (ii) from a mere nominee who has at all times, held the property on behalf of the transferee; (iii) from one nominee to another nominee of the same beneficial owner where the first nominee has at all times held the property on behalf of that beneficial owner. (NOTE - This category does not include a transfer made in any of the following circumstances: (i) by a holder of stock, etc., following the grant of an option to purchase the stock, to the person entitled to the option or his nominee; (ii) to a nominee in contemplation of a contract for the sale of the stock, etc., then about to be entered into; (iii) from the nominee of a vendor, who has instructed the nominee orally or by some unstamped writing to hold stock, etc., in trust for a purchaser, to such a purchaser.)

(1) "I" or "We".

(2) Insert "(a)" or "(b)"

(3) Here set out concisely the facts explaining the transaction Adjudication may be required.

(1) _____ hereby certify that the transaction in respect of which this transfer is made is one which falls within the category (2) _____ above.

(3)

*Signature(s)

*Description ("Transferor", "Solicitor", etc.)

Date _____ 19 _____

*NOTE - The above certificate should be signed by (1) the transferor(s) or (2) a member of a stock exchange or a solicitor or an accredited representative of a bank acting for the transferor(s); in cases falling within (a) where the bank or its official nominee is a party to the transfer, a certificate, instead of setting out the facts, may be to the effect that "the transfer is excepted from Section 74 of the Finance (1909-10) Act 1910". A certificate in other cases should be signed by a solicitor or other person (e.g. a bank) acting as trustee or executor) having a full knowledge of the facts.

JSF0018 REV: 2.0 02/98

Supplied by **Jordans Limited** Telephone 0117 923 0600

Checklist

- Ownership of shares is freely transferable, subject to any restrictions in the articles.

- A company cannot be compelled to register a transfer to a minor.

- Unless the CREST system is used, transfer must be by means of an approved stock transfer form.

- Stamp duty must be paid (by the purchaser) before the stock transfer form is submitted to the company.

- CREST is a computerised, electronic system.

- A forged transfer cannot deprive the true, registered member of his rights in the company.

- Transmission of shares occurs when a member dies, becomes bankrupt or becomes of unsound mind.

- If shares are to be transmitted, the company must take care that it deals only with persons having the correct authority. Documentation should be carefully inspected.

- If shares are held in joint names, the death of one holder results in title passing to the surviving joint holder or holders.

- A genuine share certificate issued in accordance with a company's articles is prima facie evidence of the title to the shares of the person named.

- Subject to the articles, replacement share certificates may be issued.

chapter fourteen

Receivership and administration

Introduction

Receivership

The concept of administration

The appointment of an administrator

Grounds for obtaining, and purposes of,
an administration order

Effects of administration

The early stages of administration

The later stages and conclusion of administration

Checklist

Introduction

Receivership and administration are big subjects and it is not possible to cover them completely in this chapter. There are many points not covered and a more extensive work should be consulted if this detail is needed. The law is very similar throughout the United Kingdom, but there are some differences in Scotland and Northern Ireland, compared with England and Wales. This chapter concentrates on the position in England and Wales.

Receivership and administration are grouped together because they are both governed by the Insolvency Act 1986 and the Enterprise Act 2002, and because in both cases control of the company is taken away from the directors. This power goes to an administrative receiver or an administrator. Despite the similarity in names they are not the same thing. An administrative receiver's primary function is to look after the interests of one or more secured creditors. An administrator's function is to work towards certain objectives and to do this for the benefit of the creditors as a whole. This is indirectly in the interests of the members as a whole as well. Only a Licensed Insolvency Practitioner can act as an administrative receiver or as an administrator.

A consequence of the Enterprise Act 2002 is that the use of receivership is restricted. The balance is shifted in favour of administration, which is a collective procedure and which takes into account the interests of all creditors. The Act makes administration more accessible, cheaper and less bureaucratic, and the need for a court hearing is in most cases removed.

The Enterprise Act received Royal Assent on 7th November 2002. The provisions relating to receivership and administration will take effect on a date that at the time of writing has yet to be determined. However, the date is likely to be, though not certain to be, by mid 2003. It is therefore likely that the provisions will have been implemented before this Guide is read. This chapter generally explains what the position will be after the implementation date.

Receivership

An administrative receiver is usually appointed by a debenture holder or holders, or a mortgagee. This is done by means of a deed of appointment, and it is done consequent to a breach in the terms of a debenture or mortgage. The word 'administrative' is liable to cause confusion, which is unfortunate. An administrative receiver should not be confused with an administrator. Administrators and administration orders are covered elsewhere in this chapter.

If the administrative receiver is appointed under the authority of a fixed charge, his powers only extend to the assets covered by the fixed charge. If he is appointed under the authority of a floating charge, his authority extends to all assets and he has the power to manage the business. The appointment of an administrative receiver must be registered with the registrar within seven days. It must also be published in the Gazette and an appropriate newspaper.

It is important to note that an administrative receiver's first duty is to the person or body for whom he is acting, and not to the creditors in general. The Enterprise Act 2002 curtails receivership in favour of administration. In general the holder of a floating charge may no longer appoint an administrative receiver, but there are certain exceptions to this rule. They mainly concern existing arrangements and the capital markets.

The duties of an administrative receiver, who must be a Licensed Insolvency Practitioner, are as follows:

- Formally to accept the appointment. This must be done by the end of the next working day following the appointment.

- Move to take possession of the appropriate assets.

- Obtain a statement of affairs from the directors and others who may be able to assist. This must be provided within 21 days and it is a criminal offence not to co-operate.

- Do whatever is necessary to run the business expeditiously.

- Notify the appointment to all creditors within 28 days.

- Send a report within three months, or a longer period with the permission of the court, to the registrar, all unsecured creditors of which he has knowledge and the trustees of secured creditors. He must advertise the availability of the report to genuine creditors in the same newspaper in which his appointment was advertised.

- Summon a meeting of creditors and lay his report before it.

This report must show the amount owing to the debenture holders, revealing separately the amounts of principal and interest. He must also show the amount (if any) that he expects to be available for preferential creditors, and the amount (if any) that he expects to be available for other creditors. The report should also give details of the circumstances leading to his appointment, details of his disposal of assets (including proposed disposals) and details of his conduct of the business.

When he is in a position to do so, he will repay money to the holders of a fixed charge. This must be done out of the proceeds of the specific assets charged. His own remuneration and expenses for this comes from these proceeds and ranks ahead of the payments to the holders of a fixed charge.

When he is in a position to do so he will distribute funds available as a result of a floating charge. The order of priority is as follows:

- Costs of realisation of assets.

- His own expenses and remuneration.

- Preferential creditors.

- Interest due under the terms of the debenture.

- The principal amount of the debenture.

- Any money remaining is returned to the company, or a liquidator if one has been appointed.

When this has been done the receiver should resign his appointment. The registrar must be informed within 14 days and a memorandum of satisfaction must be sent to him. The liquidator (if there is one) and the members of the creditors' committee (if there is one) must also be informed.

All the above relate to receivership in England and Wales. The position in Scotland has many similarities, but some differences.

The concept of administration

There existed for many years a general feeling that too many companies were lost that might have been rescued. A company that got into difficulties all too often went into liquidation. This happened either straight away or following receivership. A receiver's primary function was to safeguard the interests of the secured creditors that appointed him. The interests of the company and other creditors were secondary. Receivership is explained elsewhere in this chapter.

This was one of the problems addressed by the Insolvency Act 1986. The Act introduced the concept of the administration order. One of its features was an interval during which a company had protection from its creditors. This interval was to be used either to turn round the business and save all of it or part of it, or to lead to a winding up on more advantageous terms. There are of course dangers in this and safeguards are necessary, one being that the administrator must be a Licensed Insolvency Practitioner. The precise workings of administration are explained later in this chapter.

The Enterprise Act 2002 provides that an administrator will always be required, where he thinks that it is reasonably practicable, to carry out his functions with the objective of rescuing the company as a going concern.

The appointment of an administrator

Prior to the Enterprise Act 2002 the appointment of an administrator always involved an application to the court. This route into administration is still available and the application must be made by one of (or a combination of) the company, the directors, one or more creditors, or the justices' chief executive for a magistrates court (acting in respect of unpaid fines). The court will consider the application and, if it believes that a sound case has been made, it will issue an administration order.

The Enterprise Act 2002 provides out of court routes to the appointment of an administrator and it is expected that these will be more commonly used than an application to the court. The processes and safeguards are too detailed to be set out here but one of the routes may be used by the company or its directors. One condition for this is that the company is, or is likely to become, unable to pay its debts. The other route may be used by the holder of a qualifying and enforceable floating charge.

Grounds for obtaining, and purposes of, an administration order

If an application is made to the court or if the directors use the out of court route, the company must be either unable to pay its debts or likely to become unable to pay its debts. In England and Wales 'unable to pay its debts' means one of the following:

- The company has received a demand in the prescribed form for a debt of at least £750, and has not made payment for a period of at least three weeks.

- Execution or other process issued on a judgment, decree or order of any court in favour of a creditor of the company is unsatisfied in whole or in part.

- The company is unable to pay its debts as they fall due.

- The amount of the company's assets is less than that of its liabilities.

The court will only grant an administration order if it believes that there is a reasonable chance of one of the objectives listed later in this section being achieved.

If a floating charge holder uses the out of court route, he must have a qualifying and enforceable floating charge.

The purposes of administration can best be summarised by quoting part of the amended Insolvency Act 1986:

> *The administrator of a company must perform his functions with the objective of:*
>
> *a) rescuing the company as a going concern, or*
>
> *b) achieving a better result for the company's creditors as a whole than would be likely if the company were wound up (without first being in administration), or*
>
> *c) realising property in order to make a distribution to one or more secured or preferential creditors.'*

The administrator must aim to achieve the first objective unless he believes that it is not reasonably practical, or unless he believes that the second objective would achieve a better result for the company's creditors as a whole. He must only aim to achieve the third objective if he thinks that it is not reasonably practical to achieve one of the other two and that it will not unnecessarily harm the interest of the creditors as a whole.

Effects of administration

The following restrictions apply whilst administration is in progress, and they take effect from the date that the application for the administration or the notice of intention to appoint is filed at court:

- No order may be made to wind up the company or resolution passed to this effect. A winding up petition may be presented to the court, but it will not be granted whilst an application for an administration order is pending.

- No debt recovery or enforcement proceedings may be commenced. Any such proceedings that are in existence are frozen.

- Property subject to hire purchase or lease agreements may not be repossessed.

- No security may be enforced.

- No goods subject to 'retention of title' clauses may be repossessed.

The court may grant an order to override all but the first of these restrictions shown above.

The early stages of administration

An administrator is an officer of the court as well as an agent of the company and he must be a Licensed Insolvency Practitioner. During the course of the administration the restrictions listed in the previous section of this chapter continue to apply.

On appointment the administrator takes over the powers formerly exercised by the directors. He may appoint and remove directors and may call meetings of creditors and members. He has wide powers to manage the business and progress towards achievement of the object of the administration. This includes powers to borrow money, use the company seal, bring and defend actions in the name of the company and to sell company property. There are other specific powers and powers that are assumed as incidental.

The following is a summary of the new streamlined administration process:

- The administrator sends notice of his appointment to the company and to the registrar.

- Within 11 days of the appointment the directors must provide the administrator with a statement of affairs. This must include details of the company's assets, liabilities and shareholders. The administrator must file the statement of affairs with the registrar.

- The administrator must comply with notice and advertisement requirements.

- The administrator must decide which of the permitted objectives he intends to pursue.

- The administrator must produce a report setting out his proposals. This report must be sent to creditors and filed with the registrar, and this must be done within 8 weeks of his appointment unless an extended period has been granted.

The later stages and conclusion of administration

If the administrator proposes a company rescue or to realise the company's business or property, he must convene a creditors' meeting. He must give at least fourteen days notice of the meeting and it must be held within ten weeks of his appointment. However, no meeting is necessary if he proposes to realise the company's property and states that no meeting will be held unless one is requisitioned. This can be done by 10% of creditors (measured by value).

The meeting will consider the administrator's report and proposals. It may adopt the proposals, possibly with modifications. If his proposals affect the right of secured or preferential creditors to enforce their security, it can only be adopted with their consent. The proposals may be adopted by the meeting, possibly (with the consent of the administrator) with modifications. If the proposals are adopted, the administrator will work towards achieving them. A report of the outcome of the meeting must be filed by the administrator at court and with the registrar.

The administrator should conclude the administration as soon as reasonably practical, but within twelve months of its commencement. However, this period may be extended by up to six months with the consent of the creditors or for as long as necessary with the consent of the court.

The administrator is required to apply to the court to end the appointment if he thinks that the purpose of the administration cannot be achieved, that the company should not have entered into administration or if required to do so by a creditors' meeting.

Depending on the aim of the administration and the level of success achieved, control of the company may be passed back to the directors at the end of the administration. Alternatively the administrator may make what payments he can and then the company will go into liquidation.

Checklist

- Receivership and administration are big subjects. This chapter does not cover all aspects.

- The provisions of the Enterprise Act 2002 will probably, but not definitely, take effect by mid 2003. This chapter outlines the position after they have taken effect.

- Both an administrative receiver and an administrator must be a Licensed Insolvency Practitioner.

- The primary task of an administrative receiver is to look after the interests of the secured creditors who appointed him.

- The task of an administrator is to pursue an approved objective, and to safeguard the interests of creditors (and then members) as a whole.

- The Enterprise Act 2002 restricts the appointment of administrative receivers. There will be fewer receiverships and more companies placed in administration.

- An administrator must, where he thinks that it is reasonably practicable, carry out his functions with the objective of rescuing the company as a going concern.

- Administration was introduced by the Insolvency Act 1986 to promote a 'rescue culture'.

- There are now out of court routes into administration. It is expected that these will be used more commonly than an application to court.

- Steps to place a company in administration are most frequently initiated by the directors, though it can be the creditors or others.

- Administration gives a company a 'moratorium' and a period of protection from its creditors.

- An administrator must submit proposals to a meeting of creditors. The creditors may approve them, reject them, or (with the consent of the administrator) amend them.

chapter fifteen

Winding up and striking off

Introduction

Members' voluntary winding up

Creditors' voluntary winding up

Winding up by the court

The abolition of Crown Preference

Order of priority in the distribution of funds

Licensed Insolvency Practitioners

Striking off following an application by the company

Striking off at the instigation of the registrar

Checklist

Introduction

Winding up and striking off are big subjects and this chapter only has room to give an outline of the procedures. There are points of detail not covered and a more extensive work should be consulted if more than on outline is needed.

There are three types of winding up, namely:

- Members' voluntary winding up.

- Creditors' voluntary winding up.

- Winding up by the court.

The first two categories follow a decision by the members, but only the first category is under the control of the members themselves. This happens when the company is solvent. Some windings up take place because a company is insolvent and these are conducted according to the rules of one of the last two categories. Each of the three categories is examined in detail in this chapter.

The stages in all forms of winding up are as follows:

- A decision is made to wind up the company. It is made either by the members or by the court.

- A liquidator, who must be a Licensed Insolvency Practitioner, is appointed. This is done either by the members or the creditors, or it is the Official Receiver.

- The liquidator realises the assets.

- The liquidator pays out the money to the creditors in an order of precedence fixed by law. If there are funds remaining, they are returned to the contributors (members).

A further possibility is for an application to be made to the registrar to have a company struck off. This is only possible in the case of a dormant private company. Finally, a company may be struck off at the instigation of the registrar.

Members' voluntary winding up

This is the most satisfactory form of winding up and it takes place in the expectation that all creditors will be paid in full within a year. If this is not expected, the winding up should not be a members' winding up. If a winding up starts as a members' winding up, but then it is realised that all creditors may not be paid in full, control of the winding up should be passed to the creditors. As the term members' winding up implies, control of the winding up is with the company itself (the members).

An abbreviated summary of the procedure is as follows:

- The directors must make a declaration of solvency and file it with the Registrar of Companies. This must state that the directors are of the opinion that the company will be able to pay all creditors (plus interest at the official rate) within a year of commencement of the winding up.

- A general meeting of the company must be held. A special resolution to voluntarily wind up the company and appoint a liquidator must be passed.

- Within 14 days of the resolution being passed it must be published in the London Gazette (or Edinburgh Gazette in the case of a Scottish company).

- Within 15 days of the resolution being passed a copy must be filed with the registrar.

- Within 14 days of his appointment the liquidator must publish notice of his appointment in the Gazette, and must also notify the registrar. This must be done by means of form 600.

- The liquidator must realise the assets, pay off the creditors and conduct the liquidation.

- At the conclusion of the liquidation the registrar must be informed by the liquidator and the company will be removed from the register.

As the winding up is at the wish of the members, it may be done for any reason that they consider sound.

Creditors' voluntary winding up

This is like a members' voluntary winding up in that the decision is taken by the company (the members) and not by the court. However, it happens when the directors cannot make the declaration of solvency and cannot say that the company will be able to pay all creditors within a year. In these circumstances the control of the winding up is with the creditors rather than the members.

There are many similarities with a members' voluntary winding up and an abbreviated summary of the procedure is as follows:

- A meeting of the directors resolves that it is advisable to wind up the company because it cannot pay its debts as they fall due.

- A general meeting of the company is held. An extraordinary resolution to wind up the company is passed. An ordinary resolution to appoint a liquidator is passed. This is a provisional appointment and the person so appointed may be confirmed or replaced by the meeting of creditors.

- Within 14 days of the resolution being passed it must be published in the London Gazette (or Edinburgh Gazette in the case of a Scottish company).

- Within 15 days of the resolution being passed a copy must be filed with the registrar.

- A meeting of creditors must be called. At least seven days notice must be given and the meeting must be held within 14 days of the company meeting. Steps may be taken before the meeting of members to call the meeting of creditors.

- The directors must present to the meeting of creditors (to the best of their ability) a full list of creditors and the estimated amount owing to each, and a statement of affairs.

- The meeting of creditors may either confirm the liquidator appointed by the members, or it may appoint a different liquidator. If it appoints a different liquidator, its decision will prevail and the person appointed will take over the liquidation. A liquidation committee may or may not be appointed.

- Within 14 days of his appointment the liquidator must publish notice of his appointment in the Gazette, and must notify the registrar. This must be done by means of form 600.

- The liquidator realises the assets.

- The liquidator pays out the money to the creditors. This is done according to the rules of priority established by law and detailed later in this chapter.

- The liquidator prepares final accounts and statements and sends them to creditors and members. A final meeting of creditors and members is held.

- The liquidator sends the final statement to the registrar within seven days of the meeting.

- Three months later the company is dissolved and removed from the register.

Winding up by the court

A company may be wound up by the court if one of the following circumstances applies:

- The members so request it by means of a special resolution.

- The court has been petitioned by a creditor or a judgment creditor who is owed an amount of at least £750.

- Membership of a public company has fallen below two members.

- A public company has not obtained a share capital certificate within a year of registration.

- A company has not commenced trading or has stopped trading for a year.

- It is just and equitable for the company to be wound up.

The last point is a 'catchall' that gives the court wide discretion. Company secretaries with military experience may be reminded of the phrase in Queens Regulations about conduct prejudicial to good order. An example of a case where it may be used is a situation where a breakdown in trust and goodwill between the members makes company operation very difficult. By far the most common reason for a company to be wound up by the court is an inability to pay debts as they become due.

The court may be petitioned by a creditor, the members or an individual member, and in certain circumstances the Secretary of State or others. A petition may be presented to the High Court or to one of many (but not all) county courts and it must be advertised in the Gazette. The petition will be heard by the court which may reject it, or it may accept it and issue a winding up order.

Upon the issue of a winding up order, the directors are relieved of their powers and the Official Receiver becomes liquidator. The directors are required to prepare a statement of affairs within 21 days. The Official Receiver may decide not to call a meeting of creditors and to proceed with the liquidation himself. Alternatively, he may call a meeting of creditors and this meeting may choose a liquidator. A meeting of creditors must be called if one quarter of creditors, measured by value, so request it.

The liquidator, who may be the Official Receiver, will proceed with the liquidation as described in the section about a creditors' voluntary winding up. The liquidator will be under an obligation to consider the causes of the company's failure, if it has failed, and to consider the conduct of the directors and others. It is normal for him to ask creditors if there are any matters that they wish to bring to his attention. He is under a duty to report to the Department of Trade and Industry if he discovers matters that should be reported, and this may have consequences for erring directors or others.

The abolition of Crown Preference

Crown Preference is (or was) the law by which the Crown ranks as a preferential creditor in respect of certain debts owing to it. The debts affected are income tax and social security due to the Inland Revenue for 12 months and money owing to Customs and Excise (including VAT) for 6 months.

Crown Preference was abolished by the Enterprise Act 2002 which received Royal Assent on 7th November 2002. However, the date of abolition and the consequences for unsecured creditors will depend on regulations to be issued by the Secretary of State. At the time of writing, the regulations have not been issued, but it is anticipated that they will be effective by August 2003. Liquidations in progress at the date of the change will be completed in accordance with the old rules and Crown Preference will apply to them.

The ordinary creditors will always gain some of the benefits of the abolition of Crown Preference. Accordingly some of the money will be ring-fenced for them. Some of the benefits may pass to the holders of floating charges but none will pass to the remaining preferential creditors. Details of the ring fencing will depend on regulations to be issued by the Secretary of State.

Order of priority in the distribution of funds

Crown Preference was abolished by the Enterprise Act 2002, but at the time of writing the implementation date for this measure is not known. It is likely (but not certain) that implementation will be by August 2003 and the following is written on the basis that abolition has taken place. It is strongly recommended that the preceding section of this chapter be read.

One is tempted to misquote George Orwell's Animal Farm – 'all creditors are equal, but some creditors are more equal than others'. There is bound to be discontent when there is not sufficient money to pay all creditors in full, and any system of priorities will be considered unfair by some. This section sets out the law.

Secured creditors get paid out of the proceeds of their security. If the proceeds of their security are insufficient to pay them in full, they may rank as ordinary creditors for the remainder of their debts. Banks (and others) that are secured by a fixed-charge debenture are secured by the assets covered. Persons holding charging orders are secured creditors. So too are execution creditors with the benefit of walking possession agreements. Any sums realised on secured assets that are in excess of the amounts needed to pay secured creditors are available for the other creditors.

Money, other than from the proceeds of fixed securities, is applied in the following order:

- The expenses of the liquidation. This includes the liquidator's fees.

- Preferential debts (but not interest due after the liquidation).

- Debts secured by a floating charge (but not interest due after the liquidation).

- Ordinary debts (but not interest due after the liquidation).

- Interest on preferential and ordinary debts at the statutory rate.

- The contributors (members).

If funds are insufficient to pay a group in full, they will get a dividend of x pence in the pound. For example, if ordinary debts total £200,000 and only £100,000 is available, payment will be at the rate of 50p in the pound.

After the abolition of Crown Preference the main preferential debts, which rank equally between themselves, are:

- Contributions to occupational pension schemes, etc.

- Remuneration, etc, of employees – up to a period of four months and subject to a limit for each employee.

- Levies on coal and steel production.

- Money owing to third parties in connection with debts which would have been preferential had they not been paid by the third parties.

Licensed Insolvency Practitioners

Prior to the Insolvency Act 1986 almost anyone could be a liquidator and some rather unsatisfactory people did sometimes hold the position. Of course in most cases they were responsible, especially if appointed to large companies, but there were too many scandals and too many cases of incompetence. In particular there were too many cases of liquidators acting to benefit directors of failed companies.

Since 1986 a person appointed to the position of liquidator must be a Licensed Insolvency Practitioner. The licence is given by the Secretary of State, or by a person or body authorised by the Secretary of State to do so. A Licensed Insolvency Practitioner must hold one of the approved professional qualifications and be authorised by that professional body to hold the position. He must uphold professional standards and deposit an appropriate bond.

Striking off following an application by the company

Assets of a struck off company pass to the Crown and striking off will therefore be an unattractive proposition for a company having net assets. However, it is permitted to first pay a dividend to dispose of the assets. For many, striking off will be a relatively quick, easy and cheap way of terminating the registration of an unwanted company. The option is only available if the company is a private company and it must be solvent. Striking off is only suitable if a company's affairs are simple and straight forward, and, best of all, it is dormant. There are dangers if this is not the case.

Application may be made by the directors of a private company that has not, within the last three months, traded or otherwise carried on business, or changed its name. There are one or two other limitations and these are detailed in Companies House booklet GBW2. A company may not be struck off if it is the subject, or proposed subject, of insolvency proceedings or a compromise or arrangement with members or creditors.

Directors would be well advised to think carefully before applying to have a company struck off. They should check the company's obligations and contingent obligations, and it is a good idea to check in advance with anyone who might object or have an interest. Just one example of a possible problem is a contingent liability outstanding in connection with an old employment dispute.

The process starts by the directors submitting form 652a to Companies House accompanied by a fee of £10. If there is a sole director, he must sign the form and if there are two directors, both must sign. If there are more than two directors a majority of them must sign. There are certain procedures and safeguards following the application.

Striking off at the instigation of the registrar

The registrar may strike off a company that she believes is not in business or operation. She usually forms this opinion because the company does not submit accounts, an annual return or other documents, and because it ignores communications from her.

The steps to a striking off at the instigation of the registrar are as follows:

1 The registrar will write to the company at its last notified registered office. This letter will enquire if the company is still in business or operation. If no response is received or documents filed, the registrar will send a second letter by registered post.

2 If no response is received, the registrar will publish a notice in the *London Gazette* or *Edinburgh Gazette* giving notice of her intention to strike off the company.

3 The registrar will place a copy of this notice on the company's file at Companies House. This warns any enquirer of her intention.

4 The registrar will consider any representations that may be received. These may be from the company, its officers, creditors or anyone at all.

5 Not less than three months after placing the notice on the company's file at Companies House, the registrar may strike off the company.

Checklist

- This chapter is an outline summary of a big subject. Reliance should not be placed on it for more than this.

- A members' voluntary winding up may take place when the company is solvent. The decision is made by the members and the winding up is under the control of the members.

- A creditors' voluntary winding up may take place when the company is not solvent. The decision is made by the members, but the winding up is under the control of the creditors.

- A winding up may commence as a members' voluntary winding up but it may later be realised that the company is insolvent. In these circumstances control must be passed to the creditors.

- Winding up by the court is the court's decision following the hearing of a petition.

- An insolvent winding up must be under the control of the creditors or of the court.

- In the case of a winding up there is always a liquidator. He may be appointed by the members, the creditors or the court. The court's initial appointment is the Official Receiver.

- The liquidator realises the assets and pays the proceeds to the creditors. This is done according to an order of priority fixed by law. Any remaining funds go to the contributors (members).

- Secured creditors are paid from the proceeds of their security.

- The liquidator must notify the Registrar when the liquidation is complete. The company will be struck off three months later.

- If it is a winding up by the court, the liquidator must notify the Secretary of State of anything that should be brought to her attention. This applies to such matters as directors' conduct.

- Not all creditors rank equally. Full details are in this chapter.

- The liquidator must be a Licensed Insolvency Practitioner or be the Official Receiver.

- It may be possible to have a dormant private company stuck off without the expense and trouble of liquidation. Full details are in this chapter.

- The registrar may strike off a company if she believes that it is no longer in business or operation.

chapter sixteen

The annual return

Introduction

Time limits for filing the annual return

The shuttle system

The annual return in detail

Form 363A: Annual return form

List of past and present members
schedule to form 363A

Checklist

Introduction

An annual return must be filed every year for every company, including dormant companies. It confirms that the company is still in business or operation and it places on public record information that the Act requires to be in the public domain. For some information it is confirmation of what should already be on the public record. There is a filing fee (currently £15) which is the main source of income for Companies House.

The obligation to file an annual return should not be confused with the obligation to file accounts. The obligations are different and the timing requirements are also different. A shuttle annual return form is sent by the registrar each year, but a full blank form may be obtained free of charge from Companies House or downloaded from the Companies House website **www.companieshouse.gov.uk**.

The annual return must be signed by a director or the secretary and there are penalties for failure to submit timely, accurate annual returns. The annual return is an important part of the secretary's job and thus justifies a full chapter. An annual return, together with a schedule showing a list of past and present members completed with hypothetical details, is shown at the end of this chapter, just before the checklist.

Companies House has certain requirements relating to legibility and the quality of documents to be filed. It is requested that the annual return be typed or be completed in bold black capitals. The annual return may be rejected if it does not comply with minimum standards.

Time limits for filing the annual return

Two different dates are relevant:

• The date to which the annual return must be made up.

• The date by which the annual return must reach Companies House.

Formerly the annual return had to be made up to a date calculated with reference to the date of the Annual General Meeting. This is no longer the case. Instead it must be made up to a date not more than 12 months after the date to which the previous annual return was made up. In the case of a newly formed company, the first annual return must be made up to a date not more than 12 months after the date of incorporation.

It will be seen that a company may freely choose to bring forward the date of its annual return. It must merely make up the return to a date less than 12 months from the anniversary of the previous one. Provided that delivery to Companies House is made within 28 days of the new date, the effective anniversary date will be changed. If delivery to Companies House is not made within the permitted time, the attempt to change the return date will fail and it will be necessary to complete another annual return with reference to a later date.

It is not possible to put back the return date of the annual return merely by making it up to a date later than 12 months after the date to which the previous annual return was made up. This can only be achieved by filing an annual return made up to a date within the 12 month period, then filing a further return made up to a date within 12 months of this one.

The annual return must be received by Companies House within 28 days of the date to which it is made up. It should be stressed that the return must be received by Companies House, which includes its satellite offices, within 28 days. Posting within 28 days is not by itself sufficient. It is therefore good practice to request a receipt and to investigate promptly any lack of a response.

Late filing and non filing of the annual return is a criminal offence for which the directors may be fined. It is in fact the most common offence penalised by Companies House. Needless to say, it is very bad practice which may damage the reputation of a company and its officers. It may, in an extreme case, contribute to a company being struck off.

The shuttle system

It is the practice of Companies House to send a form 363s to the registered office of every company and to do so about two weeks before the anniversary of the made-up date of the last annual return. This form is pre-printed with all the relevant records on file at the time. The company may use this form as at the anniversary date or it may choose any remaining earlier date. A company may, at any time, request that an up-to-date shuttle annual return form be posted to it.

It may be necessary to deal separately with the requirement to provide details of share ownership and this is explained later. With this possible exception, it is only necessary to check that the pre-printed information is absolutely correct and up-to-date. If this is the case, the form should be signed and dated, then returned to Companies House with the filing fee of £15.

If the pre-printed information is not correct, there can be five possible reasons:

1 Companies House has recorded incorrectly information previously provided to it. This is possible but unlikely.

2 The company has made a mistake in information previously supplied to Companies House.

3 The company only very recently supplied information to Companies House and the records have not yet been updated.

4 The company has omitted to notify Companies House of a relevant change.

5 The relevant change has been so recent that the time in which Companies House should have been notified has not yet expired.

If form 363s is incorrect in any detail, it should be very neatly altered. In many respects this is all that is required. However, form 363s may not be used to update Companies House records in three areas and the appropriate form should be submitted. These three areas are:

• The appointment of a new company officer. Form 288a must be submitted for this.

• The allotment of new shares by a company. Form 88(2) must be submitted for this.

• The increase in a company's total nominal value of its share capital or an alteration in the structure of the share capital. According to what has been done it is necessary to submit one or more of form 122, form 123, form 128(1), form 128(3), form 128(4) or form 169. In some of these cases a copy of the appropriate resolution should also be submitted.

Until comparatively recently is was always necessary to submit form 288b for the termination of the appointment of a director or secretary, and to submit form 288c for a change in the notifiable details of a director or secretary. This is no longer the case and if the correct information has not already been submitted, it is only necessary to alter the shuttle annual return. Technically, the form 363s is prescribed as form 288b or form 288c.

Permitting details to be altered on the shuttle annual return is a concession. There is still an obligation to notify Companies House within the permitted time limits. In theory at least, there is still the possibility of prosecution if this is not done. However, it can be stated that in practice, other than in cases of fraud or in extremely exceptional circumstances, prosecutions will not be brought and that Companies House will act on the altered shuttle annual return.

It is obviously not good practice to fail to inform changes to Companies House as they occur. No company should want to break the law and not have its up-to-date details on file. Apart from anything else this may be bad for its reputation.

Since September 1999 Companies House has put pre-printed capital and shareholder information on shuttle annual returns for companies having up to 20 members and which have already submitted at least one previous annual return. This enables companies to update shareholder information in the same way as other details on the form. Less than 2 per cent of companies have more than 20 members. For these, Companies House will pre-print aggregate issued capital information without details of the company's members. For a small number of large companies, Companies House will not pre-print any capital information. These are companies with frequently changing information but only about 3,000 come into this category.

The use of form 363s is not compulsory. A company may choose to use the blank form 363a instead, though in practice most companies do use the shuttle form. At the time of writing an electronic shuttle document is under development but has not yet introduced.

The annual return in detail

A completed example of form 363a follows later in this chapter and, in order to illustrate the principles, specimen details have been entered. The following notes explain the form on a heading by heading basis:

Company number

This is the company's registration number. Every company has a unique registration number, which is essential because there are more than 1,500,000 companies on the active register. It must be quoted for identification purposes on all Companies House forms.

Company name in full

This must be the exact, full registered name of the company. The name of a limited company must end in 'Ltd', 'Limited', or 'Public Limited Company' or 'PLC', or the Welsh language equivalent words or abbreviations.

Date of this return

This is the date to which the return is made up and it must be not more than 12 months from the date to which the previous annual return was made up. The information on the form must be correct as at this date.

Date of next return

If this is left blank, Companies House will send a shuttle form convenient for a date 12 months hence. If an earlier date is selected, Companies House will send a shuttle form convenient for this date. The selection of an earlier date is not a binding commitment.

Registered office

The registered office was examined in detail in the chapter on the memorandum of association. Every company must have a registered office, and its location decides whether the company is governed by English law or Scottish law. Service of documents at the registered office constitutes good service. A company cannot 'go away' from its registered office. It can only change it to a different address. A change in the registered office must be notified to Companies House on form 287.

Principal business activities

There is a classification system for business activities and the company is asked to list the appropriate classification numbers. If it is unable to give these numbers, it is permitted to describe its principal activity in words.

Register of members

If this is kept at the registered office, no entry is required. If it is not kept at the registered office, location details must be given.

Register of debenture holders

If this is kept at the registered office, no entry is required. If it is not kept at the registered office, location details must be given. Of course not all companies have a register of debenture holders.

Company type

There are seven types of company listed and the correct type must be identified. The great majority of companies are private companies limited by shares. The second most numerous category is 'Private company limited by guarantee without share capital'.

Company secretary

Required details are:

- Surname

- Forenames

- Residential address

Disclosure of Style/Title (eg Miss) and Honours (eg CBE) is optional. If the address is a service address for the beneficiary of a Confidentiality Order, a box must be ticked.

Directors

Individual details are required for all directors. Required details are:

- Surname

- Forenames

- Residential address

- Business occupation

- Date of birth

- Nationality

Disclosure of Style/Title (eg Miss) and Honours (eg CBE) is optional. If the address is a service address for the beneficiary of a Confidentiality Order, a box must be ticked.

Appointment of a director, resignation or termination of a director and change of particulars for a director must be notified to Companies House on, respectively, forms 288a, 288b and 288c.

Issued share capital

This lists all the different classes of share, although many companies have just one class. It also requires the total number of shares in issue in each class, and the total nominal value of shares in issue in each class. The last two columns must be totalled to give the total number of shares issued, and the total nominal value of shares issued by the company.

List of past and present members

If the company has a share capital, a full list of past and present members is required at least once in every three annual returns. This may be submitted on the special schedule which is reproduced in this chapter. Shares acquired and disposed of since the last return must be shown as well as shares held as at the date of the return. A researcher is therefore able to follow the trail of ownership of shares, and not see just the current position.

Names and addresses of shareholders are required.

Subject to the requirement to send a full list once in every three annual returns, a list of changes may be sent and a box has to be marked to this effect. Alternatively, a box must be marked to show that there were no changes in the period.

This section of the annual return only applies to companies having a share capital. It does not apply to companies limited by guarantee.

Elective resolutions

Elective resolutions were explained in the chapter on general meetings. If either (or both) of the following types of elective resolution are in force, the appropriate box must be marked:

- an election to dispense with Annual General Meetings
- an election to dispense with laying accounts in general meetings.

Certificate

This reads 'I certify that the information given in this return is true to the best of my knowledge and belief'. The person signing takes responsibility as an individual for the truth of these words.

Signature and date

The return must be signed by a director or by the company secretary. Date means the date of signature, which is not the same thing as the date to which the return is made up.

There is a box for details of the person to be contacted by Companies House in the event of a query. This is not necessarily the same person who signed the return.

The completed form must be sent to the Registrar of Companies. This is at Cardiff for companies registered in England and Wales and at Edinburgh for companies registered in Scotland, but delivery to one of the satellite offices is acceptable. Companies House addresses are shown in Appendix C. The return must be accompanied by a payment of £15.00 and cheques should be made payable to 'Companies House'.

Companies House
—— *for the record* ——
*Please complete in typescript,
or in bold black capitals.*
CHFP000

363a

Annual Return

Company Number | 1611842

Company Name in full | Wendover Alarms Limited

Date of this return
The information in this return is made up to

Day	Month	Year
3 0	0 4	2 0 0 3

Date of next return
If you wish to make your next return to a date earlier than the anniversary of this return please show the date here. Companies House will then send a form at the appropriate time.

Day   Month   Year

Registered Office
Show here the address at **the date of this return.**

66 Claydon Road

Any change of registered office **must** *be notified on form 287.*

Post town | Wendover

County / Region | Buckinghamshire

UK Postcode | H P 2 2   4 T F

SPECIMEN

Principal business activities
Show trade classification code number(s) for the principal activity or activities.

If the code number cannot be determined, give a brief description of principal activity.

Installation and service of Burglar alarms

Companies House receipt date barcode

This form has been provided free of charge by Companies House

Form April 2002

When you have completed and signed the form please send it to the Registrar of Companies at:

Companies House, Crown Way, Cardiff, CF14 3UZ   **DX 33050 Cardiff**
for companies registered in England and Wales
or
Companies House, 37 Castle Terrace, Edinburgh, EH1 2EB
for companies registered in Scotland   **DX 235 Edinburgh**

Page 1

Register of members

If the register of members is not kept at the registered office, state here where it is kept.

Smith and Benson (Chartered Accountants)

187 Church Square

Post town | Aylesbury

County / Region | Buckinghamshire | UK Postcode | H P 1 8 9 L P

Register of Debenture holders

If there is a register of debenture holders, or a duplicate of any such register or part of it, which is not kept at the registered office, state here where it is kept.

Post town

County / Region | UK Postcode

Company type

Public limited company ☐

Private company limited by shares ☒

Private company limited by guarantee without share capital ☐

Private company limited by shares exempt under section 30 ☐

Private company limited by guarantee exempt under section 30 ☐

Private unlimited company with share capital ☐

Private unlimited company without share capital ☐

Please tick the appropriate box

SPECIMEN

Company Secretary

* Voluntary details.

(Please photocopy this area to provide details of joint secretaries).

†† Tick this box if the address shown is a service address for the beneficiary of a Confidentiality Order granted under section 723B of the Companies Act 1985 otherwise, give your usual residential address. In the case of a corporation or Scottish firm, give the registered or principal office address.

If a partnership give the names and addresses of the partners or the name of the partnership and office address.

Details of a new company secretary must be notified on form 288a.

Name

* Style / Title | Mrs

Forename(s) | Charlotte

Surname | Lewis

Address †† | 66 Claydon Road

Post town | Wendover

County / Region | Buckinghamshire | UK Postcode | H P 2 2 4 T F

Country | England

Directors

Please list directors in alphabetical order.

Details of new directors must be notified on form 288a

Directors In the case of a director that is a corporation or a Scottish firm, the name is the corporate or firm name.

†† Tick this box if the address shown is a service address for the beneficiary of a Confidentiality Order granted under section 723B of the Companies Act 1985 otherwise, give your usual residential address. In the case of a corporation or Scottish firm, give the registered or principal office address.

Name   * Style / Title   Mr

Date of birth   Day 2 4   Month 0 7   Year 1 9 3 9

Forename(s)   Charles Peter

Surname   Lewis

Address ††   66 Claydon Road

Post town   Wendover

County / Region   Buckinghamshire   UK Postcode   H P 2 2   4 T F

Country   England   **Nationality**   British

Business occupation   Service Engineer

* Voluntary details.

Directors In the case of a director that is a corporation or a Scottish firm, the name is the corporate or firm name.

†† Tick this box if the address shown is a service address for the beneficiary of a Confidentiality Order granted under section 723B of the Companies Act 1985 otherwise, give your usual residential address. In the case of a corporation or Scottish firm, give the registered or principal office address.

Name   * Style / Title   Mrs

Date of birth   Day 2 4   Month 0 8   Year 1 9 5 2

Forename(s)   Charlotte

Surname   Lewis

Address ††   66 Claydon Road

Post town   Wendover

County / Region   Buckinghamshire   UK Postcode   H P 2 2   4 T F

Country   England   **Nationality**   German

Business occupation   Administrator

SPECIMEN

	Class (e.g. Ordinary/Preference)	Number of shares issued	Aggregate Nominal Value (i.e Number of shares issued multiplied by nominal value per share, or total amount of stock)
Issued share capital Enter details of all the shares in issue at the date of this return.			
	Ordinary 20p	50,000	£10,000.00
	Totals	50,000	£10,000.00

List of past and present shareholders
(Use attached schedule where appropriate)
A full list is required if one was not included with either of the last two returns.

There were no changes in the period ☐

	on paper	in another format
A list of changes is enclosed	☐	☐
A full list of shareholders is enclosed	☒	☐

SPECIMEN

Certificate

I certify that the information given in this return is true to the best of my knowledge and belief.

Signed *Charlotte Lewis*   **Date** 4th May 2003

† Please delete as appropriate.

† a director /secretary

When you have signed the return send it with the fee to the Registrar of Companies. Cheques should be made payable to **Companies House.**

This return includes   0   continuation sheets.
(enter number)

You do not have to give any contact information in the box opposite but if you do, it will help Companies House to contact you if there is a query on the form. The contact information that you give will be visiable to searchers of the public record.

Mrs C Lewis

66 Claydon Road, Wendover, Buckinghamshire

HP22 4TF   Tel 01296 622118

DX number   DX exchange

Directors

Please list directors in alphabetical order.

Details of new directors must be notified on form 288a

Directors In the case of a director that is a corporation or a Scottish firm, the name is the corporate or firm name.

†† Tick this box if the address shown is a service address for the beneficiary of a Confidentiality Order granted under section 723B of the Companies Act 1985 otherwise, give your usual residential address. In the case of a corporation or Scottish firm, give the registered or principal office address.

Name * Style / Title	Mr
Date of birth	Day 1 9 / Month 0 2 / Year 1 9 6 7
Forename(s)	Michael Anthony
Surname	Smith
Address ††	77 Clinton Road
Post town	Aylesbury
County / Region	Buckinghamshire UK Postcode H P 1 9 . 6 B L D
Country	England **Nationality** British
Business occupation	Chartered Accountant

SPECIMEN

* Voluntary details.

Directors In the case of a director that is a corporation or a Scottish firm, the name is the corporate or firm name.

†† Tick this box if the address shown is a service address for the beneficiary of a Confidentiality Order granted under section 723B of the Companies Act 1985 otherwise, give your usual residential address. In the case of a corporation or Scottish firm, give the registered or principal office address.

Name * Style / Title	
Date of birth	Day / Month / Year
Forename(s)	
Surname	
Address ††	
Post town	
County / Region	UK Postcode
Country	**Nationality**
Business occupation	

Directors

Please list directors in alphabetical order.

Details of new directors must be notified on form 288a

Name * Style / Title

Directors In the case of a director that is a corporation or a Scottish firm, the name is the corporate or firm name.

Day   Month   Year

Date of birth   └─ └─ / └─ └─ / └─ └─ └─ └─

Forename(s)

†† Tick this box if the address shown is a service address for the beneficiary of a Confidentiality Order granted under section 723B of the Companies Act 1985 otherwise, give your usual residential address. In the case of a corporation or Scottish firm, give the registered or principal office address.

Surname

Address ††

Post town

County / Region   UK Postcode └─ └─ └─ └─   └─ └─ └─

Country   **Nationality**

Business occupation

* Voluntary details.

Name * Style / Title

Directors In the case of a director that is a corporation or a Scottish firm, the name is the corporate or firm name.

Day   Month   Year

Date of birth   └─ └─ / └─ └─ / └─ └─ └─ └─

Forename(s)

†† Tick this box if the address shown is a service address for the beneficiary of a Confidentiality Order granted under section 723B of the Companies Act 1985 otherwise, give your usual residential address. In the case of a corporation or Scottish firm, give the registered or principal office address.

Surname

Address ††

Post town

County / Region   UK Postcode └─ └─ └─ └─   └─ └─ └─

Country   **Nationality**

Business occupation

SPECIMEN

Companies House
for the record

List of past and present shareholders
Schedule to form 363a

CHFP000

Company Number 1611842

Company Name in full Wendover Alarms Limited

➤ Changes to shareholders particulars or details of the amount of stock or shares transferred must be completed each year

➤ You must provide a "full list" of all the company shareholders on:
- The company's first annual return following incorporation;
- Every third annual return after a full list has been provided

➤ List the company shareholders in alphabetical order or provide an ind

➤ List joint shareholders consecutively

Shareholders' details	Class and number of shares or amount of stock held	Shares or amount of stock transferred *(if appropriate)*	
		Class and number of shares or amount of stock transferred	Date of registration of transfer
Name Mr C P Lewis Address 66 Claydon Road Wendover Buckinghamshire UK Postcode H P 2 2 4 T F	Ordinary 20p 46,000		
Name Mrs C Lewis Address 66 Claydon Road Wendover Buckinghamshire UK Postcode H P 2 2 4 T F	Ordinary 20p 3,000	Ordinary 20p 1,000 disposed of	03.01.03
Name Mr K Lewis Address 31 Flower Street Nottingham UK Postcode N G 1 4 2 L R	Ordinary 20p 1,000	Ordinary 20p 1,000 acquired	03.01.03

SPECIMEN

9/99

Checklist

- An annual return must be filed every year for every company.

- The obligation to file an annual return is different from the obligation to file accounts. The timing requirements are different too.

- A shuttle annual return (form 363s) is sent out by the registrar in good time for the anniversary of the made up date of the last return.

- The annual return must be made up to a date not later than 12 months after the date to which the last annual return was made up. This period may be shortened but it may not be lengthened.

- The annual return must reach Companies House within 28 days of the date to which it is made up.

- Late filing and non filing are criminal offences.

- A full list of shareholders must accompany the annual return at least every third submission. For other submissions only details of changes need be sent. This only applies to companies having a share capital.

- Acquisitions and disposals of shares must be disclosed. This is as well as membership details at the date to which the return is made up.

- Certain details (eg appointment of a new director) must be notified to Companies House when they happen. It is not correct to do this only on the annual return.

- Companies House has certain requirements relating to legibility and document quality. A return may be rejected if these requirements are not met.

chapter seventeen

Dealing with Companies House

Introduction

Companies House forms

Requirements to file resolutions

Quality of documents filed at Company House

Penalties and prosecutions in connection with late and non-filing

Obtaining information from Companies House

Methods of filing

Checklist

Introduction

Companies House affects all companies and all company directors. Especially, it affects all company secretaries. In practice it is usually the company secretary who ensures that the company complies with regulations concerning the filing of forms and other documents. Of course there is more to it than this. A good company secretary should be able to answer questions from and about Companies House, and should be able to use Companies House creatively for the benefit of his company. In particular he should know what information is available and how to obtain it.

In the context of this chapter, the Registrar of Companies means the same thing as Companies House. An obligation to file documents at Companies House means an obligation to file documents with the Registrar of Companies. Companies House is an Executive Agency of the Department of Trade and Industry. It issues a very helpful set of guidance notes, which are listed in Appendix C, and in the experience of the writer, its staff are very helpful. In the words of one of its guidance notes, it has five main functions:

- The registration of new companies.

- The registration of documents required to be delivered under companies, insolvency and related legislation.

- The provision of company information to the public.

- Dissolution and striking off companies from the register.

- Ensuring that companies comply with their obligations in connection with above functions.

Three of the appendices to this book concern Companies House and the statutory forms. These appendices, which are well worth an inspection, are:

- **Appendix C: Companies House contact details and guidance booklets**

- **Appendix D: Examples of completed Companies House** forms – these are some of the main forms most likely to be of interest to company secretaries. They have been completed with hypothetical details in order to illustrate the principles.

- **Appendix E: Full list of Companies House forms**.

Companies House forms

There are a considerable number of Companies House forms, the full list being shown in Appendix E. In particular, the annual return should not be overlooked and the whole of Chapter 16 is devoted to it. Each form is numbered according to the section of the Act to which it relates. For example, form 287 notifies Companies House of a change in the situation or address of the registered office. Section 287 of the Act is devoted to the registered office.

All the forms may be obtained free of charge from Companies House, and they may be downloaded from the Companies House website. Companies House will provide the forms to personal callers or will post them in response to a telephone request. The full list of Companies House addresses is shown in Appendix C. For companies registered in England and Wales, the completed forms should be sent to Cardiff. For companies registered in Scotland, the completed forms should be sent to Edinburgh. Both Cardiff and Edinburgh addresses are shown on each form. In the experience of the writer, Companies House staff are very helpful and are willing to respond to a reasonable telephone query about a form, or indeed to any reasonable query.

The forms have the following in common:

* They require the exact, registered company name to be shown in full.

* The company number must be shown. This is the unique, registered number allocated to each company by Companies House. There are over 1,500,000 registered companies and it is important for identification purposes.

* All forms must be signed and each form identifies the category of person who may do so. Many forms must be signed by a director or the company secretary.

* All forms request the name and contact details of a person who may be contacted in the event of a query about the form. This need not be the person who signs it.

Appendix D reproduces a selection of the most frequently used forms. In order to illustrate the principles, each one has been completed with hypothetical details.

Requirements to file resolutions

Copies of certain resolutions must be filed at Companies House within 15 days of them being passed. Not all resolutions need be filed but the following is a summary of the ones that must:

Special, extraordinary and elective resolutions (of members) and resolutions to cancel elective resolutions

Copies of all such resolutions must be filed and so must resolutions passed by unanimous agreement of all members that would otherwise have needed to be passed as such resolutions.

Class resolutions (of members)

- Class resolutions passed by unanimous agreement of all the holders of a class of share but which would otherwise have needed to be passed by a specific majority or in another manner. Also, all resolutions or agreements that effectively bind all the holders of any class of share though they have not been agreed by all those holders.

Ordinary resolutions (of members)

- a resolution to give, vary, revoke or renew an authority to the directors to allot shares.

- a resolution to give, vary, revoke or renew an authority to the company to make a market purchase of its own shares.

- a resolution to prevent or reverse a directors' resolution to allow title of shares to be evidenced or transferred without a written document.

- a resolution to authorise an increase of share capital. This type of resolution must be sent with form 123 (notice of increase in nominal capital).

Directors' resolutions

- a resolution to change the company's name in response to a direction from the Secretary of State under section 31(2) of the Companies Act 1985.

- a resolution to alter the memorandum of association of a company ceasing to be a public company following the acquisition of its own shares.

- a resolution by the directors of an old public company to re-register as a plc.

- a resolution to allow title (meaning the right to benefit from ownership) to be evidenced and transferred without a written document.

Companies House has standard forms for companies wishing to change their name and for dormant companies exempting themselves from the requirement to appoint an auditor. With these exemptions (which are in any case voluntary) forms for resolutions are not available and the resolutions must be filed on plain paper. Each resolution filed must be certified by a competent person. It is usual for the certification to be done by the chairman of the meeting that passed the resolution, but it can be done by the company secretary or a director.

Quality of documents filed at Companies House

Companies House requirements may just occasionally appear irritating but there are sound reasons for their requests and requirements. Company secretaries will appreciate the reasons when they need to inspect information filed. Companies House is permitted to reject documents that do not meet the required quality standards and to issue a notice requiring their replacement within 14 days.

All documents are converted to a visual image and the quality must be such that this can be satisfactorily achieved. Companies House requirements are:

- Every document must state prominently the company's registered number. This should normally appear in the top right hand corner and a box is provided on all pre-printed forms.

- Documents must be on paper which is white or otherwise of a background density not greater than 0.3.

- Documents must be on paper with a matt finish.

- Each page must be on A4 size paper.

- Each page must have a margin all round not less than 10mm wide. If the document is bound, the bound edge must have a margin of not less than 20mm.

- Letters must be clear, legible, and of uniform density.

- Letters and numbers must be not less than 1.8mm high, with a line width of not less than 0.25mm.

- Letters and numbers must be black or otherwise providing reflected line density of not less than 1.0.

Companies House requires that documents are completed in black ink or black type. Bold capital letters are preferred (but not demanded) for written documents. A possible source of problems is the glossy finish of annual accounts which do not conform with the requirement for matt finish. Most accountants understand the requirements and produce matt finish for Companies House, even if it is glossy for the shareholders, the media and the coffee table.

Facsimile signatures are now accepted. It is, of course, an offence to use a facsimile signature without the consent of the person concerned.

Penalties and prosecutions in connection with late and non-filing

Time limits apply to all documents that must by law be filed at Companies House. Many of the forms must be filed within 14 days of the relevant event. For example, this is the time limit for the appointment of a director or secretary, the resignation of a director or secretary or a change of particulars for a director or secretary. These events must be notified on forms 288a, 288b and 288c respectively which are the most used of the Companies House forms.

Criminal prosecutions may be brought against directors and in some cases others, if filing is late or does not take place. In practice, prosecution of directors is the most common. Prosecutions may be under the control of Companies House or the Department of Trade and Industry. Involvement of the Department of Trade and Industry is more likely if fraud is suspected, or if the offence is serious, blatant or wilful.

Of course, Companies House will not bring a prosecution every time a form comes in late, which is just as well. They are unlikely to do so if the delay is short, no complaint is made and there are no apparent harmful consequences. They more likely to do so if the delay is protracted, a complaint is made or they are aware of problems caused by the failure.

They are much more likely to do so if they suspect fraud or wilful abuse, or in the case of repeated negligence. In practice the number of prosecutions is small and an innocent mistake is very unlikely to be punished in this way.

A further possible consequence should be mentioned. Non-filing, particularly of accounts and the annual return, may lead the registrar to believe that the company is no longer in business or operation. As a consequence she may instigate steps that result in the company being struck off the register. Considerable expense and inconvenience may result.

Late filing of company accounts is treated differently. Section 242A of the Act provides for automatic late filing penalties on the company. It is possible that directors could be prosecuted individually as well as the company obliged to pay a late filing penalty, though it does not often happen. The penalties apply to all companies, big and small, and are applied automatically. Companies House has only a very little discretion in the matter. Discretion is exercised only in very exceptional circumstances. Late filing penalties only apply to accounts, not to other documents, and they are a civil penalty, not a criminal matter.

The scale of the penalties is as follows:

	Public company	Private company
Not more than three months late	£500	£100
More than three months late but not more than six months late	£1,000	£250
More than six months late but not more than 12 months late	£2,000	£500
More than 12 months late	£5,000	£1,000

The accounts of a public company must be filed within seven months of the accounting reference date, and the accounts of a private company must be filed within ten months of the accounting reference date. Filed means actually received by Companies House. Merely posting by the due date is not sufficient. The periods of seven months and ten months run from the day in the month, which can cause confusion and ill-feeling. For example, accounts made up to 28 February must be filed by 28 September in the case of a public company and 28 December in the case of a private company. In both cases a three months extension may be claimed if the company has exports or overseas interests. The extension may be claimed by the directors by sending form 244 to Companies House before the accounts are overdue.

Companies House does not automatically acknowledge accounts, forms and documents sent to it for filing. However, it will do so if they are accompanied by a stamped addressed envelope and a letter in duplicate requesting a receipt. This is a wise precaution for accounts and other documents where timing is particularly important.

Obtaining information from Companies House

Most of this chapter and all of the last chapter deal with a company's obligations to provide information for Companies House. These obligations are obviously important for the company secretary and form a significant part of his job. The obligation to file information is imposed because it is deemed to be in the public interest that it be placed in the public domain. This especially applies to limited companies where public disclosure is deemed to be a necessary consequence of the privilege of limited liability.

It should not be overlooked that all this information is available to company secretaries and others. It is possible to obtain information about rival companies or indeed about any company. This may be done for commercial reasons, including a safeguard when credit is granted, but it may be done for any reason at all, including just curiosity.

With the exception of residential addresses covered by confidentiality orders, everything that goes to Companies House is available. The trail of information can be followed, so earlier filings can be seen as well as the current information. The following is an outline summary of what is available:

1 **The memorandum and articles of association**
   These are covered in Chapters 9 and 10.

2 **The annual return**
   This is covered in Chapter 16.

3 **Accounts**
   This is covered in Chapter 4.

4 **Resolutions**

These are explained in this chapter.

5 **Directors and company secretary**

Details are advised on forms 288a, 288b and 288c, and the information is confirmed annually on the annual return. Notifiable information is obtainable from the record of each company and it is also possible to make a director-based enquiry.

6 **The forms**

This is covered in this chapter and a full list of the forms is given in Appendix E.

7 **Disqualified Directors Register**

This is an up to date list of the names and certain other details of all persons currently banned by the court from acting as a director.

8 **The Company Names and Address Index**

This is a list of the exact names of all companies currently on the active register together with key information about each company.

9 **Entities other than companies incorporated in Great Britain under the Companies Acts**

Companies incorporated in Great Britain under the Companies Acts constitute the great majority of bodies that file at Companies House, but other entities must file too. An examination of the forms listed in Appendix E will indicate which types of organisation must do so.

Information may be obtained by the following methods:

By personal application

This may be to any of the six Information Centres listed in Appendix C.

The information is available on microfiche, but the service has been greatly improved and extended by the introduction of a Windows-based system and terminals can be used to access a wide range of information from the database. All documents filed since 1995 have been scanned electronically. Electronic images of these documents can be viewed on the screens and hard copies of them printed if so wished. The terminals may be used for a range of other things as well as viewing and printing documents.

The method of payment for the on-line information is to purchase a pre-paid card for any amount chosen. It works rather like a telephone card. The use of the various services uses up the amount that has been pre-paid and eventually the sum is exhausted. At this point a further card can be purchased. Some of the information is free and a card is not necessary for it. There is always a charge for printing a document.

Telephone, post or fax

Orders for copies of company documents may be made by telephone, post or fax, but in practice telephone is likely to be the most convenient. If an account has not been opened, it is necessary to supply credit card details or pay in advance.

Copies of documents or microfiches are normally dispatched by first class post. As long as an order is received by 3.00pm, It will normally be dispatched on the same day. If an order is received after 3.00pm, it will normally be dispatched on the following working day. If a customer requests that a document be faxed, the fax will normally be sent on the day that the order is received (perhaps after normal office hours), as long as the order is received by 4.00pm.

Companies House website

Certain information is available free of charge on the Companies House website **www.companieshouse.gov.uk**

Monitor

This service provides exactly what the name suggests. It monitors specified companies and provides copies of pre-ordered documents as soon as they are filed. This can be done in an ad hoc way or on a continuing basis. Pre-payment is required or an account may be opened.

CD-ROMs

A CD-ROM is published monthly and may be purchased (current price £30). The following information is included for all live companies incorporated in Great Britain, companies in liquidation or receivership, and companies dissolved, converted or closed within the proceeding 12 months:

- Company name

- Registered company number

- Registered office address

- Accounting reference date

- Date of the latest annual return filed

- Date of latest accounts filed

- Accounts type

- Date of information

- Company type

- Company status

- Trade classification

- Mortgage indicator

- Postcode

Companies House Direct

This is an on-line service that offers the user the best, quickest and most flexible way of accessing information registered at Companies House. It is very attractive to large users such as credit reference agencies and it enables the Companies House database to be accessed from a PC. The main features of the service are:

- Options to view on-line or downloaded images of documents that have been registered since March 1995

- A directors' database that can be searched on an individual or company basis

- A mortgage register providing information on the charges for any chosen company

- Documents and microfiche ordering facilities

- Free basic company details and disqualified directors index

- Available 17 hours a day, Monday to Saturday

- Context-sensitive on-line help facilities

- A link to the Companies House website

Methods of filing

The methods are as follows:

1 By post

This is still the most common method of filing. Documents relating to companies incorporated in England and Wales should be posted to Cardiff. Documents relating to companies incorporated in Scotland should be posted to Edinburgh.

2 Hays document exchange

This service is available only to those registered to use it.

3 By personal delivery or courier

All offices can accept documents delivered by hand 24 hours a day. Cardiff provides a manned reception desk but at the other offices delivery is via letterboxes.

4 Electronic filing

Electronic filing was introduced in 1998, initially just for a few forms. At first take up was slow but its use is now rapidly expanding. Companies House intends that by 2005 it will be possible for all documents to be filed electronically. This includes accounts and resolutions – not just forms.

Electronic filing is available to subscribers to the service who have registered for the purpose.

Checklist

- Companies House issues very helpful guidance notes. These are available free of charge and are listed by subject in Appendix C.

- Appendices C, D and E relate to Companies House.

- A full list of Companies House forms is shown in Appendix E. The annual return is covered in Chapter 16.

- Each form is numbered according to the section of the Act to which it relates.

- All forms may be obtained free of charge from Companies House.

- Facsimile and photocopied signatures are now accepted by Companies House. It is an offence to submit such a signature without the consent of the person concerned.

- Certain resolutions must be filed and full details are in this chapter. With just two exceptions, no forms are available for this purpose.

- Companies House has requirements relating to document quality and documents may be rejected if they do not meet the requirements. Full details are in this chapter.

- Time limits apply to the filing of all documents. There are automatic civil penalties if accounts are filed late. Prosecution of the directors is possible in all cases of late filing, though in practice prosecutions are rare.

- Electronic filing is becoming more common.

- It is intended that by 2005 it will be possible to file all documents (including accounts) electronically.

- With the exception of a residential address which is the subject of a confidentially order, all information filed at Companies House is available for inspection.

appendix A

Table A to the Companies Act 1985

Regulations for management of a
company limited by shares

Regulations for management of a company limited by shares

Interpretation

1. In these regulations:

    *   "the Act" means the Companies Act 1985 including any statutory modification or re-enactment thereof for the time being in force.

    *   "the articles" means the articles of the company.

    *   "clear days" in relation to the period of a notice means that period excluding the day when the notice is given or deemed to be given and the day for which it is given or on which it is to take effect.

    *   "executed" includes any mode of execution.

    *   "office" means the registered office of the company.

    *   "the holder" in relation to shares means the member whose name is entered in the register of members as the holder of the shares.

    *   "the seal" means the common seal of the company.

    *   "secretary" means the secretary of the company or any other person appointed to perform the duties of the secretary of the company, including a joint, assistant or deputy secretary.

    *   "the United Kingdom" means Great Britain and Northern Ireland.

    *   "communication" means the same as in the Electronic Communications Act 2000.

    *   "electronic communication" means the same as in the Electronic Communications Act 2000.

    *   Unless the context otherwise requires, words or expressions contained in these regulations bear the same meaning as in the Act but including any statutory modification thereof not in force when these regulations become binding on the company.

Share capital

2. Subject to the provisions of the Act and without prejudice to any rights attached to any existing shares, any share may be issued with such rights or restrictions as the company may by ordinary resolution determine.

3. Subject to the provisions of the Act, shares may be issued which are to be redeemed or are to be liable to be redeemed at the option of the company or the holder on such terms and in such manner as may be provided by the articles.

4. The company may exercise the powers of paying commissions conferred by the Act. Subject to the provisions of the Act, any such commission may be satisfied by the payment of cash or by the allotment of fully or partly paid shares or partly in one way and partly in the other.

5. Except as required by law, no person shall be recognised by the company as holding any share upon any trust and (except as otherwise provided by the articles or by law) the company shall not be bound by or recognise any interest in any share except an absolute right to the entirety thereof in the holder.

Share certificates

6. Every member, upon becoming the holder of any shares, shall be entitled without payment to one certificate for all the shares of each class held by him (and, upon transferring a part of his holding of shares of any class, to a certificate for the balance of such holding) or several certificates each for one or more of his shares upon payment for every certificate after the first of such reasonable sum as the directors may determine. Every certificate shall be sealed with the seal and shall specify the number, class and distinguishing numbers (if any) of the shares to which it relates and the amount or respective amounts paid up thereon. The company shall not be bound to issue more than one certificate for shares held jointly by several persons and delivery of a certificate to one joint holder shall be a sufficient delivery to all of them.

7.   If a share certificate is defaced, worn-out, lost or destroyed, it may be renewed on such terms (if any) as to evidence and indemnity and payment of the expenses reasonably incurred by the company in investigating evidence as the directors may determine but otherwise free of charge, and (in the case of defacement or wearing-out) on delivery up of the old certificate.

Lien

8.   The company shall have a first and paramount lien on every share (not being a fully paid share) for all moneys (whether presently payable or not) payable at a fixed time or called in respect of that share. The directors may at any time declare any share to be wholly or in part exempt from the provisions of this regulation. The company's lien on a share shall extend to any amount payable in respect of it.

9.   The company may sell in such manner as the directors determine any shares on which the company has a lien if a sum in respect of which the lien exists is presently payable and is not paid within fourteen clear days after notice has been given to the holder of the share or to the person entitled to it in consequence of the death or bankruptcy of the holder, demanding payment and stating that if the notice is not complied with the shares may be sold.

10.   To give effect to a sale the directors may authorise some person to execute an instrument of transfer of the shares sold to, or in accordance with the directors of, the purchaser. The title of the transferee to the shares shall not be affected by any irregularity in or invalidity of the proceedings in reference to the sale.

11.   The net proceeds of the sale, after payment of the costs, shall be applied in payment of so much of the sum for which the lien exists as is presently payable, and any residue shall (upon surrender to the company for cancellation of the certificate for the shares sold and subject to a like lien for any moneys not presently payable as existed upon the shares before the sale) be paid to the person entitled to the shares at the date of the sale.

Call on shares and forfeiture

12. Subject to the terms of allotment, the directors may make calls upon the members in respect of any moneys unpaid on their shares (whether in respect of nominal value or premium) and each member shall (subject to receiving at least fourteen clear days' notice specifying when and where payment is to be made) pay to the company as required by the notice the amount called on his shares. A call may be required to be paid by instalments. A call may, before receipt by the company of any sum due thereunder, be revoked in whole or part and payment of a call may be postponed in whole or part. A person upon whom a call is made shall remain liable for calls made upon him notwithstanding the subsequent transfer of the shares in respect whereof the call was made.

13. A call shall be deemed to have been made at the time when the resolution of the directors authorising the call was passed.

14. The joint holders of a share shall be jointly and severally liable to pay all calls in respect thereof.

15. If a call remains unpaid after it has become due and payable the person from whom it is due and payable shall pay interest on the amount unpaid from the day it became due and payable until it is paid at the rate fixed by the terms of allotment of the share or in the notice of the call or, if no rate is fixed, at the appropriate rate (as defined by the Act) but the directors may waive payment of the interest wholly or in part.

16. An amount payable in respect of a share on allotment or at any fixed date, whether in respect of nominal value or premium or as an instalment of a call, shall be deemed to be a call and if it is not paid the provisions of the articles shall apply as if that amount had become due and payable by virtue of a call.

17. Subject to the terms of the allotment, the directors may make arrangements on the issue of shares for a difference between the holders in the amounts and times of payments of calls on their share.

18. If a call remains unpaid after it has become due and payable the directors may give to the person from whom it is due not less than fourteen clear days' notice requiring payment of the amount unpaid together with any interest which may have accrued. The notice shall name the place where payment is to be made and shall state

that if the notice is not complied with the shares in respect of which the call was made will be liable to be forfeited.

19. If the notice is not complied with any share in respect of which it was given may, before the payment required by the notice has been made, be forfeited by a resolution of the directors and the forfeiture shall include all dividends or other moneys payable in respect of the forfeited shares and not paid before the forfeiture.

20. Subject to the provisions of the Act, a forfeited share may be sold, re-allotted or otherwise disposed of on such terms and in such manner as the directors determine either to the person who was before the forfeiture the holder or to any other person and at any time before sale, re-allotment or other disposition, the forfeiture may be cancelled on such terms as the directors think fit. Where for the purpose of its disposal a forfeited share is to be transferred to any person the directors may authorise some person to execute an instrument of transfer of the share to that person.

21. A person any of whose shares have been forfeited shall cease to be a member in respect of them and shall surrender to the company for cancellation the certificate for the shares forfeited but shall remain liable to the company for all moneys which at the date of forfeiture were presently payable by him to the company in respect of those shares with interest at the rate at which interest was payable on those moneys before the forfeiture or, if no interest was so payable, at the appropriate rate (as defined in the Act) from the date of forfeiture until payment but the directors may waive payment wholly or in part or enforce payment without any allowance for the value of the shares at the time of forfeiture or for any consideration received on their disposal.

22. A statutory declaration by a director or the secretary that a share has been forfeited on a specified date shall be conclusive evidence of the facts stated in it as against all persons claiming to be entitled to the share and the declaration shall (subject to the execution of an instrument of transfer if necessary) constitute a good title to the share and the person to whom the share is disposed of shall not be bound to see to the application of the consideration, if any, nor shall his title to the share be affected by any irregularity in or invalidity of the proceedings in reference to the forfeiture or disposal of the share.

Transfer of shares

23. The instrument of transfer of a share may be in any usual form or in any other form which the directors may approve and shall be executed by or on behalf of the transferor and, unless the share is fully paid, by or on behalf of the transferee.

24. The directors may refuse to register the transfer of a share which is not fully paid to a person of whom they do not approve and they may refuse to register the transfer of a share on which the company has a lien. They may also refuse to register a transfer unless:

    a) it is lodged at the office or at such other place as the directors may appoint and is accompanied by the certificate of the shares to which it relates and such other evidence as the directors may reasonably require to show the right of the transferor to make the transfer.

    b) it is in respect of only one class of shares; and

    c) it is in favour of not more than four transferees.

25. If the directors refuse to register a transfer of a share, they shall within two months after the date on which the transfer was lodged with the company send to the transferee notice of the refusal.

26. The registration of transfers of shares or of transfers of any class of shares may be suspended at such times and for such periods (not exceeding thirty days in any year) as the directors may determine.

27. No fee shall be charged for the registration of any instrument of transfer or other document relating to or affecting the title to any share.

28. The company shall be entitled to retain any instrument of transfer which is registered, but any instrument of transfer which the directors refuse to register shall be returned to the person lodging it when notice of the refusal is given.

Transmission of shares

29. If a member dies the survivor or survivors where he was a joint holder, and his personal representatives where he was a sole holder or the only survivor of joint holders, shall be the only persons recognised by the company as having any title to his interest; but nothing herein contained shall release the estate of a deceased member from any liability in respect of any share which had been jointly held by him.

30. A person becoming entitled to a share in consequence of the death or bankruptcy of a member may, upon such evidence being produced as the directors may properly require, elect either to become the holder of the share or to have some person nominated by him registered as the transferee. If he elects to become the holder he shall give notice to the company to that effect. If he elects to have another person registered he shall execute an instrument of transfer of the share to that person. All the articles relating to the transfer of shares shall apply to the notice of instrument of transfer as if it were an instrument of transfer executed by the member and the death or bankruptcy of the member had not occurred.

31. A person becoming entitled to a share in consequence of the death or bankruptcy of a member shall have the rights to which he would be entitled if he were the holder of the share, except that he shall not, before being registered as the holder of the share, be entitled in respect of it to attend or vote at any meeting of the company or at any separate meeting of the holders of any class of shares in the company.

Alteration of share capital

32. The company may by ordinary resolution:

a) increase its share capital by new shares of such amount as the resolution prescribes;

b) consolidate and divide all or any of its share capital into shares of larger amount than its existing shares;

c) subject to the provisions of the Act sub-divide its shares, or any of them, into shares of smaller amount and the resolution may determine that, as between the shares resulting from the sub-division, any of them may have any preference or advantage as compared with the others, and

d) cancel shares which, at the date of the passing of the resolution, have not been taken or agreed to be taken by any person and diminish the amount of its share capital by the amount of the shares so cancelled.

33. Whenever as a result of a consolidation of shares any members would become entitled to fractions of a share, the directors may, on behalf of those members, sell the shares representing the fractions for the best price reasonably obtainable to any person (including, subject to the provisions of the Act, the company) and distribute the net proceeds of sale in due proportion among those members, and the directors may authorise some person to execute an instrument of transfer of the shares to, or in accordance with the directions of, the purchaser. The transferee shall not be bound to see to the application of the purchase money nor shall his title to the shares be affected by any irregularity in or invalidity of the proceedings in reference to the sale.

34. Subject to the provisions of the Act, the company may by special resolution reduce its share capital, any capital redemption reserve and any share premium account in any way.

Purchase of own shares

35. Subject to the provisions of the Act, the company may purchase its own shares (including any redeemable shares) and, if it is a private company, make a payment in respect of the redemption or purchase of its own shares otherwise than out of distributable profits of the company or the proceeds of a fresh issue of shares.

General Meetings

36. All general meetings other than annual general meetings shall be called extraordinary general meetings.

37. The directors may call general meetings and, on the requisition of members pursuant to the provisions of the Act, shall forthwith proceed to convene an extraordinary general meeting for a date not later than eight weeks after receipt of the requisition. If there are not within the United Kingdom sufficient directors to call a general meeting, any director or any member of the company may call a general meeting.

Notice of General Meetings

38. An annual general meeting and an extraordinary general meeting called for the passing of a special resolution or a resolution appointing a person as a director shall be called by at least twenty-one clear days' notice. All other extraordinary general meetings shall be called by at least fourteen clear day's notice but a general meeting may be called by shorter notice if it is so agreed:

   a) in the case of an annual general meeting, by all the members entitled to attend and vote thereat; and

   b) in the case of any other meeting by a majority in number of the members having a right to attend and vote being a majority together holding not less than ninety-five per cent in nominal value of the shares giving that right.

   The notice shall specify the time and place of the meeting and the general nature of the business to be transacted and, in the case of an annual general meting, shall specify the meeting as such.

   Subject to the provision of the articles and to any restrictions imposed on any shares, the notice shall be given to all the members, to all persons entitled to a share in consequence of the death or bankruptcy of a member and to the directors and auditors.

39. The accidental omission to give notice of a meeting to, or the non-receipt of notice of a meeting by, any person entitled to receive notice shall not invalidate the proceedings at that meeting.

Procedures at General Meetings

40. No business shall be transacted at any meeting unless a quorum is present. Two persons entitled to vote upon the business to be transacted, each being a member or a proxy for a member or a duly authorised representative of a corporation, shall be a quorum.

41. If such a quorum is not present within half an hour from the time appointed for the meeting, or if during a meeting such a quorum ceases to be present, the meeting shall stand adjourned to the same day in the next week at the same time and place or to such time and place as the directors may determine.

42. The chairman, if any, of the board of directors or in his absence some other director nominated by the directors shall preside as chairman of the meeting, but if neither the chairman nor such other director (if any) be present within fifteen minutes after the time

appointed for holding the meeting and willing to act, the directors present shall elect one of their number to be chairman and, if there is only one director present and willing to act, he shall be chairman.

43. If no director is willing to act as chairman, or if no director is present within fifteen minutes after the time appointed for holding the meeting, the members present and entitled to vote shall choose one of their number to be chairman.

44. A director shall, notwithstanding that he is not a member, be entitled to attend and speak at any general meeting and at any separate meeting of the holders of any class of shares in the company.

45. The chairman may, with the consent of a meeting at which a quorum is present (and shall if so directed by the meeting), adjourn the meeting from time to time and from place to place, but no business shall be transacted at an adjourned meeting other than business which might properly have been transacted at the meeting had the adjournment not taken place. When a meeting is adjourned for fourteen days or more, at least seven clear days' notice shall be given specifying the time and place of the adjourned meeting and the general nature of the business to be transacted. Otherwise it shall not be necessary to give any such notice.

46. A resolution put to the vote of a meeting shall be decided on a show of hands unless before, or on the declaration of the result of, the show of hands a poll is duly demanded. Subject to the provisions of the Act, a poll may be demanded:

a) by the chairman; or

b) by at least two members having the right to vote at the meeting; or

c) by a member or members representing not less than one-tenth of the total voting rights of all the members having the right to vote at the meeting; or

d) by a member or members holding shares conferring a right to vote at the meeting being shares on which an aggregate sum has been paid up equal to not less than one-tenth of the total sum paid up on all the shares conferring that right;

and a demand by a person as proxy for a member shall be the same as a demand by the member.

47. Unless a poll is duly demanded a declaration by the chairman that a resolution has been carried or carried unanimously, or by a particular majority, or lost, or not carried by a particular majority and an entry to that effect in the minutes of the meeting shall be conclusive evidence of the fact without proof of the number or proportion of the votes recorded in favour of or against the resolution.

48. The demand for a poll may, before the poll is taken, be withdrawn but only with the consent of the chairman and a demand so withdrawn shall not be taken to have invalidated the result of a show of hands declared before the demand was made.

49. A poll shall be taken as the chairman directs and he may appoint scrutineers (who need not be members) and fix a time and place for declaring the result of the poll. The result of the poll shall be deemed to be the resolution of the meeting at which the poll was demanded.

50. In the case of an equality of votes, whether on a show of hands or on a poll, the chairman shall be entitled to a casting vote in addition to any other vote he may have.

51. A poll demanded on the election of a chairman or on a question of adjournment shall be taken forthwith. A poll demanded on any other question shall be taken either forthwith or at such time and place as the chairman directs not being more than thirty days after the poll was demanded. The demand for a poll shall not prevent the continuance of a meeting for the transaction of any business other than the question on which the poll was demanded. If a poll is demanded before the declaration of the result of a show of hands and the demand is duly withdrawn, the meeting shall continue as if the demand had not been made.

52. No notice need be given of a poll not taken forthwith if the time and place at which it is to be taken are announced at the meeting at which it is demanded. In any other case at least seven clear days' notice shall be given specifying the time and place at which the poll is to be taken.

53. A resolution in writing executed by or on behalf of each member who would have been entitled to vote upon it if it had been proposed at a general meeting at which he was present shall be as effectual as if it had been passed at a general meeting duly convened and held and may consist of several instruments in the like form each executed by or on behalf of one or more members.

Votes of members

54. Subject to any rights or restrictions attached to any shares, on a show of hands every member who (being an individual) is present in person or (being a corporation) is present by a duly authorised representative, not being himself a member entitled to vote, shall have one vote and on a poll every member shall have one vote for every share of which he is the holder.

55. In the case of joint holders the vote of the senior who tenders a vote, whether in person or by proxy, shall be accepted to the exclusion of the votes of the other joint holders; and seniority shall be determined by the order in which the names of the holders stand in the register of members.

56. A member in respect of whom an order has been made by any court having jurisdiction (whether in the United Kingdom or elsewhere) in matters concerning mental disorder may vote, whether on a show of hands or on a poll, by his receiver, curator bonis or other person authorised in that behalf appointed by that court, and any such receiver, curator bonis or other person may, on a poll, vote by proxy. Evidence to the satisfaction of the directors of the authority of the person claiming to exercise the right to vote shall be deposited at the office, or at such other place as is specified in accordance with the articles for the deposit of instruments of proxy, not less than 48 hours before the time appointed for holding the meeting or adjourned meeting at which the right to vote is to be exercised and in default the right to vote shall not be exerciseable.

57. No member shall vote at any general meeting or at any separate meeting of the holders of any class of shares in the company, either in person or by proxy, in respect of any shares held by him unless all moneys presently payable by him in respect of that share have been paid.

58. No objection shall be raised to the qualification of any voter except at the meeting or adjourned meeting at which the vote objected to is tendered, and every vote not disallowed at the meeting shall be valid. Any objection made in due time shall be referred to the chairman whose decision shall be final and conclusive.

59. On a poll votes may be given either personally or by proxy. A member may appoint more than one proxy to attend on the same occasion.

60. The appointment of a proxy, executed by or on behalf of the appointor shall be in the following form (or in a form as near thereto as circumstances allow or in any other form which is usual or which the directors may approve):

"

PLC/Limited

I/We,   , of

, being a

member/members of the above-named company, hereby appoint

of

,or failing him,

of   , as my/our proxy to vote in my/our name(s) and on my/our behalf at the annual/extraordinary general meeting of the company to be held on   19 , and at any adjournment thereof.

Signed on   19   ."

61. Where it is desired to afford members an opportunity of instructing the proxy how he shall act the appointment of a proxy shall be in the following form (or in a form as near thereto as circumstances allow or in any other form which is usual or which the directors may approve):

"

PLC/Limited

I/We,   , of

, being a

member/members of the above-named company, hereby appoint

of

,or failing him,

of   , as my/our proxy to vote in my/our name(s) and on my/our behalf at the annual/extraordinary general meeting of the company to be held on   19 , and at any adjournment thereof.

This form is to be used in respect of the resolutions mentioned below as follows:

Resolution No. 1 *for *against

Resolution No. 2 *for *against

*Strike out whichever is not desired.

Unless otherwise instructed, the proxy may vote as he thinks fit or abstain from voting.

Signed this   day of   19   ."

62. The appointment of a proxy and any authority under which it is executed or a copy of such authority certified notarially or in some other way approved by the directors may:

a) in the case of an instrument in writing be deposited at the office or at such other place within the United Kingdom as is specified in the notice convening the meeting or in any instrument of proxy sent out by the company in relation to the meeting not less than 48 hours before the time for holding the meeting or adjourned meeting at which the person named in the instrument proposes to vote; or

   i) In the case of an appointment contained in an electronic communication, where an address has been specified for the purpose of receiving electronic communications:

      1) in the notice convening the meeting, or

      2) in any instrument of proxy sent out by the company in relation to the meeting, or

      3) in any invitation contained in an electronic communication to appoint a proxy issued by the company in relation to the meeting.

be received at such address not less than 48 hours before the time for holding the meeting or adjourned meeting at which the person named in the appointment proposes to vote.

b) in the case of a poll taken more than 48 hours after it is demanded, be deposited or received as aforesaid after the poll has been demanded and not less than 24 hours before the time appointed for the taking of the poll; or

c) where the poll is not taken forthwith but is taken not more than 48 hours after it was demanded, be delivered at the meeting at which the poll was demanded to the chairman or to the secretary or to any director:

and an appointment of proxy which is not deposited, delivered or received in a manner so permitted shall be invalid. In this regulation and the next "address" in relation to electronic communications, includes any number or address used for the purpose of such communications.

63. A vote given or poll demanded by proxy or by the duly authorised representative of a corporation shall be valid not withstanding the previous determination of the authority of the person voting or demanding a poll unless notice of the determination was received by the company at the office or at such other place at which the instrument of proxy was duly deposited or, where the appointment of the proxy was contained in an electronic communication, at the address at which such appointment was duly received for the commencement of the meeting or adjourned meeting at which the vote is given or the poll demanded or (in the case of a poll taken otherwise than on the same day as the meeting or adjourned meeting) the time appointed for taking the poll.

Number of directors

64. Unless otherwise determined by ordinary resolution, the number of directors (other than alternate directors) shall not be subject to any maximum but shall be not less than two.

Alternate directors

65. Any director (other than an alternate director) may appoint any other director, or any other person approved by resolution of the directors and willing to act, to be an alternate director and may remove from office an alternate director so appointed by him.

66. An alternate director shall be entitled to receive notice of all meetings of directors and of all meetings of committees of directors of which his appointor is a member, to attend and vote at any such meeting at which the director appointing him is not personally present, and generally to perform all the functions of his appointor as a director in his absence but shall not be entitled to receive any remuneration from the company for his services as an alternate director. But it shall not be necessary to give notice of such a meeting to an alternate director who is absent from the United Kingdom.

67. An alternate director shall cease to be an alternate director if his appointor ceases to be a director; but, if a director retires by rotation or otherwise but is reappointed or deemed to have been reappointed at the meeting at which he retires, any appointment of an alternate director made by him which was in force immediately prior to his retirement shall continue after his reappointment.

68. Any appointment or removal of an alternate director shall be by notice to the company signed by the director making or revoking the appointment or in any other manner approved by the directors.

69. Save as otherwise provided in the articles, an alternate director shall be deemed for all purposes to be a director and shall alone be responsible for his own acts and defaults and he shall not be deemed to be the agent of the director appointing him.

Powers of directors

70. Subject to the provisions of the Act, the memorandum and the articles and to any directions given by special resolution, the business of the company shall be managed by the directors who may exercise all the powers of the company. No alteration of the memorandum or articles and no such direction shall invalidate any prior act of the directors which would have been valid if that alteration had not been made or that direction had not been given. The powers given by this regulation shall not be limited by any special power given to the directors by the articles and a meeting of directors at which a quorum is present may exercise all powers exercisable by the directors.

71. The directors may, by power of attorney or otherwise, appoint any person to be the agent of the company for such purposes and on such conditions as they determine, including authority for the agent to delegate all or any of his powers.

Delegation of directors' powers

72. The directors may delegate any of their powers to any committee consisting of one or more directors. They may also delegate to any managing director or any director holding any other executive office such of their powers as they consider desirable to be exercised by him. Any such delegation may be made subject to any conditions the directors may impose, and either collaterally with or to the exclusion of their own powers and may be revoked or altered. Subject to any such conditions, the proceedings of a committee with two or more members shall be governed by the articles regulating the proceedings of directors so far as they are capable of applying.

Appointment and retirement of directors

73. At the first annual general meeting all the directors shall retire from office, and at every subsequent annual general meeting one-third of the directors who are subject to retirement by rotation or, if their number is not three or a multiple of three, the number nearest to one-third shall retire from office; but, if there is only one director who is subject to retirement by rotation, he shall retire.

74. Subject to the provisions of the Act, the directors to retire by rotation shall be those who have been longest in office since their last appointment or reappointment, but as between persons who became or were last reappointed directors on the same day those to retire shall (unless they otherwise agree among themselves) be determined by lot.

75. If the company, at the meeting at which a director retires by rotation, does not fill the vacancy the retiring director shall, if willing to act, be deemed to have been reappointed unless at the meeting it is resolved not to fill the vacancy or unless a resolution for the reappointment of the director is put to the meeting and lost.

76. No person other than a director retiring by rotation shall be appointed or reappointed a director at any general meeting unless:

    a) he is recommended by the directors; or

    b) not less than fourteen nor more than thirty-five clear days before the date appointed for the meeting, notice executed by a member qualified to vote at the meeting has been given to the company of the intention to propose that person for appointment or reappointment stating the particulars which would, if he were so appointed or reappointed, be required to be included in the company's register of directors together with notice executed by that person of his willingness to be appointed or reappointed.

77. Not less than seven nor more than twenty-eight clear days before the date appointed for holding a general meeting notice shall be given to all who are entitled to receive notice of the meeting of any person (other than a director retiring by rotation at the meeting) who is recommended by the directors for appointment or reappointment as a director at the meeting or in respect of whom notice has been duly given to the company of the intention to propose him at the meeting for appointment or reappointment as a director. The notice shall give the particulars of that person which would, if he were so appointed or reappointed, be required to be included in the company's register of directors.

78. Subject as aforesaid, the company may by ordinary resolution appoint a person who is willing to act to be a director either to fill a vacancy or as an additional director and may also determine the rotation in which any additional directors are to retire.

79. The directors may appoint a person who is willing to act to be a director, either to fill a vacancy or as an additional director, provided that the appointment does not cause the number of directors to exceed any number fixed by or in accordance with the articles as the maximum number of directors. A director so appointed shall hold office only until the next following annual general meeting and shall not be taken into account in determining the directors who are to retire by rotation at the meeting. If not reappointed at such annual general meeting, he shall vacate office at the conclusion thereof.

80. Subject as aforesaid, a director who retires at an annual general meeting may, if willing to act, be reappointed. If he is not reappointed, he shall retain office until the meeting appoints someone in his place or if it does not do so, until the end of the meeting.

Disqualification of directors

81. The office of a director shall be vacated if:

    a) he ceases to be a director by virtue of any provision of the Act or he becomes prohibited by law from being a director; or

    b) he becomes bankrupt or makes any arrangement or composition with his creditors generally; or

    c) he is, or may be, suffering from mental disorder and either:

        i) he is admitted to hospital in pursuance of an application for admission for treatment under the Mental Health Act 1983 or, in Scotland, an application for admission under the Mental Health (Scotland) Act 1960, or

        ii) an order is made by a court having jurisdiction (whether in the United Kingdom or elsewhere) in matters concerning mental disorder for his detention or for the appointment of a receiver, curator bonis or other person to exercise powers with respect to his property or affairs; or

    d) he resigns his office by notice to the company; or

    e) he shall for more than six consecutive months have been absent without permission of the directors from meetings of directors held during that period and the directors resolve that his office be vacated.

Remuneration of directors

82. The directors shall be entitled to such remuneration as the company may by ordinary resolution determine and, unless the resolution provides otherwise, the remuneration shall be deemed to accrue from day to day.

Directors' expenses

83. The directors may be paid all travelling, hotel, and other expenses properly incurred by them in connection with their attendance at meetings of directors or committees of directors or general meetings or separate meetings of the holders of any class of shares or of debentures of the company or otherwise in connection with the discharge of their duties.

Directors' appointments and interests

84. Subject to the provisions of the Act, the directors may appoint one or more of their number to the office of managing director or to any other executive office under the company and may enter into an agreement or arrangement with any director for his employment by the company or for the provision by him of any services outside the scope of the ordinary duties of a director. Any such appointment, agreement or arrangement may be made upon such terms as the directors determine and they may remunerate any such director for his services as they think fit. Any appointment of a director to an executive office shall terminate if he cease to be a director but without prejudice to any claim to damages for breach of the contract of service between the director and the company. A managing director and a director holding any other executive office shall not be subject to retirement by rotation.

85. Subject to the provisions of the Act, and provided that he has disclosed to the directors the nature and extent of any material interest of his, a director notwithstanding his office:

a) may be a party to, or otherwise interested in, any transaction or arrangement with the company or in which the company is otherwise interested;

b) may be a director or other officer of, or employed by, or a party to any transaction or arrangement with, or otherwise interested in, any body corporate promoted by the company or in which the company is otherwise interested; and

c) shall not, by reason of his office, be accountable to the company for any benefit which he derives from any such office or employment or from any transaction or arrangement or from any interest in any such body corporate and no such transaction or arrangement shall be liable to be avoided on the ground of any such interest or benefit.

86. For the purposes of regulation 85:

    a) a general notice given to the directors that a director is to be regarded as having an interest of the nature and extent specified in the notice in any transaction or arrangement in which a specified person or class of persons is interested shall be deemed to be a disclosure that the director has an interest in any such transaction of the nature and extent so specified; and

    b) an interest of which a director has no knowledge and of which it is unreasonable to expect him to have knowledge shall not be treated as an interest of his.

Directors' gratuities and pensions

87. The directors may provide benefits, whether by the payment of gratuities or pensions or by insurance or otherwise, for any director who has held but no longer holds any executive office or employment with the company or with any body corporate which is or has been a subsidiary of the company or a predecessor in business of the company or of any such subsidiary, and for any member of his family (including a spouse and a former spouse) or any person who is or was dependent on him, and may (as well before as after he ceases to hold such office or employment) contribute to any fund and pay premiums for the purchase of provision of any such benefit.

Proceedings of directors

88. Subject to the provisions of the articles, the directors may regulate their proceedings as they think fit. A director may, and the secretary at the request of a director shall, call a meeting of the directors. It shall not be necessary to give notice of a meeting to a director who is absent from the United Kingdom. Questions arising at a meeting shall be decided by a majority of votes. In the case of an equality of votes, the chairman shall have a second or casting vote. A director who is also an alternate director shall be entitled in the absence of his appointor to a separate vote on behalf of his appointor in addition to his own vote.

89. The quorum for the transaction of the business of the directors may be fixed by the directors and unless so fixed at any other number shall be two. A person who holds office only as an alternate director shall, if his appointor is not present, be counted in the quorum.

90. The continuing directors or a sole continuing director may act notwithstanding any vacancies in their number, but, if the number of directors is less than the number fixed as a quorum, the continuing directors or director may act only for the purpose of filling vacancies or of calling a general meeting.

91. The directors may appoint one of their number to be the chairman of the board of directors and may at any time remove him from that office. Unless he is unwilling to do so, the director so appointed shall preside at every meeting of directors at which he is present. But if there is no director holding that office, or if the director holding it is unwilling to preside or is not present within five minutes after the time appointed for the meeting, the directors present may appoint one of their number to be chairman of the meeting.

92. All acts done by a meeting of directors, or of a committee of directors, or by a person acting as a director shall, notwithstanding that it be afterwards discovered that there was a defect in the appointment of any director or that any of them were disqualified from holding office, or had vacated office, or were not entitled to vote, be as valid as if every such person had been duly appointed and was qualified and had continued to be a director and had been entitled to vote.

93. A resolution in writing signed by all the directors entitled to receive notice of a meeting of directors or of a committee of directors shall be as valid and effectual as if it had been passed at a meeting of directors or (as the case may be) a committee of directors duly convened and held and may consist of several documents in the like form each signed by one or more directors; but a resolution signed by an alternate director need not also be signed by his appointor and, if it is signed by a director who has appointed an alternate director, it need not be signed by the alternate director in that capacity.

94. Save as otherwise provided by the articles, a director shall not vote at a meeting of directors or of a committee of directors on any resolution concerning a matter in which he has, directly or indirectly, an interest or duty which is material and which conflicts or may conflict with the interests of the company unless his interest or duty arises only because the case falls within one or more of the following paragraphs:

    a) the resolution relates to the giving to him of a guarantee, security, or indemnity in respect to money lent to, or an obligation incurred by him for the benefit of, the company or any of its subsidiaries:

    b) the resolution relates to the giving to a third party of a guarantee, security, or indemnity in respect of an obligation of the company or any of its subsidiaries for which the director has assumed responsibility in whole or part and whether alone or jointly with others under a guarantee or indemnity or by the giving of security;

    c) his interest arises by virtue of his subscribing or agreeing to subscribe for any shares, debenture or other securities of the company or any of its subsidiaries, or by virtue of his being, or intending to become, a participant in the underwriting or sub-underwriting of an offer of any such shares, debentures, or other securities by the company or any of its subsidiaries for subscription, purchase or exchange;

    d) the resolution relates in any way to a retirement benefits scheme which has been approved, or is conditional upon approval, by the Board of Inland Revenue for taxation purposes.

    For the purposes of this regulation, an interest of a person who is, for any purpose of the Act (excluding any statutory modification thereof not in force when this regulation becomes binding on the company), connected with a director shall be treated as an interest of the director and, in relation to an alternate director, an interest of his appointor shall be treated as an interest of the alternate director without prejudice to any interest which the alternate director has otherwise.

95. A director shall not be counted in the quorum present at a meeting in relation to a resolution on which he is not entitled to vote.

96. The company may by ordinary resolution suspend or relax to any extent, either generally or in respect of any particular matter, any provision of the article prohibiting a director from voting at a meeting of directors or of a committee of directors.

97. Where proposals are under consideration concerning the appointment of two or more directors to offices or employment with the company or any body corporate in which the company is interested the proposals may be divided and considered in relation to each director separately and (provided he is not for another reason precluded from voting) each of the directors convened shall be entitled to vote and be counted in the quorum in respect of each resolution except that concerning his own appointment.

98. If a question arises at a meeting of directors or of a committee of directors as to the right of a director to vote, the question may, before the conclusion of the meeting, be referred to the chairman of the meeting and his ruling in relation to any director other than himself shall be final and conclusive.

Secretary

99. Subject to the provisions of the Act, the secretary shall be appointed by the directors for such term, at such remuneration and upon such conditions as they may think fit; and any secretary so appointed may be removed by them.

Minutes

100. The directors shall cause minutes to be made in books kept for the purpose:

    a) of all appointments of officers made by the directors; and

    b) of all proceedings at meetings of the company, of the holder of any class of shares in the company, and of the directors, and of committees of directors, including the names of the directors present at each such meeting.

The seal

101. The seal shall only be used by the authority of the directors or of a committee of directors authorised by the directors. The directors may determine who shall sign any instrument to which the seal is affixed and unless otherwise so determined it shall be signed by a director and by the secretary or by a second director.

Dividends

102. Subject to the provisions of the Act, the company may by ordinary resolution declare dividends in accordance with the respective rights of the members, but no dividend shall exceed the amount recommended by the directors.

103. Subject to the provisions of the Act, the directors may pay interim dividends if it appears to them that they are justified by the profits of the company available for distribution. If the share capital is divided into different classes, the directors may pay interim dividends on shares which confer deferred or non-preferred rights with regard to dividend as well as on shares which confer preferential rights with regard to dividend, but no interim dividend shall be paid on shares carrying deferred or non-preferred rights if, at the time of payment, any preferential dividend is in arrear. The directors may also pay at intervals settled by them any dividend payable at a fixed rate if it appears to them that the profits available for distribution justify the payment. Provided the directors act in good faith they shall not incur any liability to the holders of shares conferring preferred rights for any loss they may suffer by the lawful payment of an interim dividend on any shares having deferred or non-preferred rights.

104. Except as otherwise provided by the rights attached to shares, all dividends shall be declared and paid according to the amounts paid up on the shares on which the dividend is paid. All dividends shall be apportioned and paid proportionately to the amounts paid up on the shares during any portion or portions of the period in respect of which the dividend is paid; but, if any share is issued on terms providing that it shall rank for dividend as from a particular date, that share shall rank for dividend accordingly.

105. A general meeting declaring a dividend may, upon the recommendation of the directors, direct that it shall be satisfied wholly or partly by the distribution of assets and, where any difficulty arises in regard to the distribution, the directors may settle the same and in particular may issue fractional certificates and fix the value for distribution of any assets and may determine that cash shall be paid to any member upon the footing of the value so fixed in order to adjust the rights of members and may vest any assets in trustees.

106. Any dividend or other moneys payable in respect of a share may be paid by cheque sent by post to the registered address of the person entitled or, if two or more persons are the holders of the share or are jointly entitled to it by reason of the death or bankruptcy of the holder, to the registered address of that one of those persons who is first named in the register of members or to such person and to such address as the person or persons entitled may in writing direct. Every cheque shall be made payable to the order of the person or persons entitled or to such other person as the person or persons entitled may in writing direct and payment of the cheque shall be a good discharge to the company. Any joint holder or other person jointly entitled to a share as aforesaid may give receipts for any dividend or other moneys payable in respect of the share.

107. No dividend or other moneys payable in respect of a share shall bear interest against the company unless otherwise provided by the rights attached to the share.

108. Any dividend which has remained unclaimed for twelve years from the date when it became due for payment shall, if the directors so resolve, be forfeited and cease to remain owing by the company.

Accounts

109. No member shall (as such) have any right of inspecting any accounting records or other book or document of the company except as conferred by statute or authorised by the directors or by ordinary resolution of the company.

Capitalisation of profits

110. The directors may with the authority of an ordinary resolution of the company:

a) subject as hereinafter provided, resolve to capitalise any undivided profits of the company not required for paying any preferential dividend (whether or not they are available for distribution) or any sum standing to the credit of the company's share premium account or capital redemption reserve;

b) appropriate the sum resolved to be capitalised to the members who would have been entitled to it if it were distributed by way of dividend and in the same proportions and apply such sum on their behalf either in or towards paying up the amounts, if any, for the time being unpaid on any shares held by them respectively, or in paying up in full unissued shares or debentures of the company of a nominal amount equal to that sum, and allot the shares or debentures credited as fully paid to those members, or as they may direct, in those proportions, or partly in one way and partly in the other, but the share premium account, the capital redemption reserve, and any profits which are not available for distribution may, for the purposes of this regulation, only be applied in paying up unissued shares to be allotted to members credited as fully paid;

c) make such provision by the issue of fractional certificates or by payment in cash or otherwise as they determine in the case of shares or debentures becoming distributable under this regulation in fractions; and

d) authorise any person to enter on behalf of all the members concerned into an agreement with the company providing for the allotment to them respectively, credited as fully paid, of any shares or debentures to which they are entitled upon such capitalisation, any agreement made under such authority being binding on all such members.

Notices

111. Any notice to be given to or by any person pursuant to the articles (other than a notice calling a meeting of the directors) shall be in writing or shall be given using electronic communications to an address for the time being notified for that purpose to the person giving the notice.

    In this regulation, "address" in relation to electronic communications, includes any number or address used for the purposes of such communications.

112. The company may give any notice to a member either personally or by sending it by post in a prepaid envelope addressed to the member at his registered address or by leaving it at that address or by giving it using electronic communications to an address for the time being notified to the company by the member. In the case of joint holders of a share, all notices shall be given to the joint holder whose name stands first in the register of members in respect of the joint holding and notice so given shall be sufficient notice to all the joint holders. A member whose registered address is not within the United Kingdom and who gives to the company an address within the United Kingdom at which notices may be given to him, or an address to which notices may be sent using electronic communications, shall be entitled to have notices given to him at that address, but otherwise no such member shall be entitled to receive any notice from the company. In this regulation and the next, "address", in relation to electronic communications, includes any number or address used for the purposes of such communications.

113. A member present, either in person or by proxy, at any meeting of the company or of the holders of any class of shares in the company shall be deemed to have received notice of the meeting and, where requisite, of the purpose for which it was called.

114. Every person who becomes entitled to a share shall be bound by any notice in respect of that share which, before his name is entered in the register of members, has been duly given to a person from whom he derives his title.

115. Proof that an envelope containing a notice was properly addressed, prepaid and posted shall be conclusive evidence that the notice was given. Proof that a notice contained in an electronic communication was sent in accordance with guidance issued by the Institute of Chartered Secretaries and Administrators shall be conclusive evidence that the notice was given. A notice shall be deemed to be given at the expiration of 48 hours after the envelope containing it was posted or, in the case of a notice contained in an electronic communication, at the expiration of 48 hours after the time it was sent.

116. A notice may be given by the company to the persons entitled to share in consequence of the death or bankruptcy of a member by sending or delivering it, in any manner authorised by the articles for the giving of notice to a member, addressed to them by name, or by the title of representatives of the deceased, for trustee of the bankrupt or by any like description at the address if any, within the United kingdom supplied for that purpose by the persons claiming to be so entitled. Until such an address has been supplied, a notice may be given in any manner in which it might have been given if the death or bankruptcy had not occurred.

Winding up

117. If the company is wound up, the liquidator may, with the sanction of an extraordinary resolution of the company and any other sanction required by the Act, divide among the members in specie the whole or any part of the assets of the company and may, for that purpose, value any assets and determine how the division shall be carried out as between the members or different classes of members. The liquidator may, with the like sanction, vest the whole or any part of the assets in trustees upon such trusts for the benefit of the members as he with the like sanction determines, but no member shall be compelled to accept any assets upon which there is a liability.

Indemnity

118. Subject to the provisions of the Act but without prejudice to any indemnity to which a director may otherwise be entitled, every director or other officer or auditor of the company shall be indemnified out of the assets of the company against any liability incurred by him in defending any proceedings, whether civil or criminal, in which judgement is given in his favour or in which he is acquitted or in connection with any application in which relief is granted to him by the court from liability for negligence, default, breach of duty or breach of trust in relation to the affairs of the company.

appendix B

Table C to the Companies Act 1985

Regulations for management of a company limited
by guarantee and not having a share capital

Regulations for management of a company limited by guarantee and not having a share capital

Note

The regulations are reproduced in full below. Table C takes Table A as a base, but deletes or amends individual regulations within it. Therefore Table A, to the extent that it is not amended by Table C, applies to a company limited by guarantee and not having a share capital. It is therefore necessary to refer to Table A when studying Table C. Table C is as follows:

Preliminary

1.   Regulations 2 to 35 inclusive, 54, 55, 57, 59, 102 and 108 inclusive, 110, 114, 116 and 117 of Table A, shall not apply to the company but the articles hereinafter contained and, subject to the modifications hereinafter expressed, the remaining regulations of Table A shall constitute the articles of association of the company.

Interpretation

2.   In regulation 1 of Table A, the definition of 'the holder' shall be omitted.

Members

3.   The subscribers to the memorandum of association of the company and such other persons as are admitted to membership in accordance with the articles shall be members of the company. No person shall be admitted a member of the company unless he is approved by the directors. Every person who wishes to become a member shall deliver to the company an application for membership in such form as the directors require executed by him.

4.   A member may at any time withdraw from the company by giving at least seven clear days' notice to the company. Membership shall not be transferable and shall cease on death.

Table C to the Companies Act 1985

appendix B

Notice of General Meeting

5. In regulation 38 of Table A:

   a) in paragraph (b) the words 'of the total voting rights at the meeting of all the members' shall be substituted for 'in nominal value of the shares giving that right' and

   b) the words 'The notice shall be given to all the members and to the directors and auditors' shall be substituted for the last sentence.

Proceedings at General Meetings

6. The words 'and at any separate meeting of the holders of any class of shares in the company' shall be omitted from regulation 44 of Table A.

7. Paragraph (d) of regulation 46 of Table A shall be omitted.

Votes of Members

8. On a show of hands every member present in person shall have one vote. On a poll every member present in person or by proxy shall have one vote.

Directors' Expenses

9. The words 'if any class of shares or' shall be omitted from regulation 83 of Table A.

Proceedings of Directors

10. In paragraph (c) of regulation 94 of Table A the word 'debentures' shall be substituted for the words 'shares, debenture or other securities' in both places where they occur.

Minutes

11. The words 'of the holders of any class of shares in the company' shall be omitted from regulation 100 of Table A.

Notices

12. The second sentence of regulation 112 of Table A shall be omitted.

13. The words 'or of the holders of any class of shares in the company' shall be omitted from regulation 113 of Table A.

appendix C

Companies House details and guidance booklets

Company House addresses

Companies House guidance booklets

Company House addresses

Cardiff

Crown Way

Maindy

Cardiff

Central Enquiries Tel: 0870 33 33 636

Switchboard: (029) 2038 8588

Opening Hours: 8.30am to 5.00pm

London

21 Bloomsbury Street

London

WC1B 3XD

Tel: 0870 33 33 636

Opening times: 9.00am to 5.00pm

Edinburgh

37 Castle Terrace

Edinburgh

EH1 2EB

Tel 0870 33 33 636

Opening times: 9.00am to 5.00pm

Website address

The Companies House website is **www.companieshouse.gov.uk**

Companies House guidance booklets

The booklets are available from any Companies House office and they are reproduced on the Companies House Web Site: **www.companieshouse.gov.uk**:

Formation and registration

Company Formation	GBF1
Company Names	GBF2
Business Names	GBF3

Administration and Management

Directors and Secretaries Guide	GBA1
Annual Return	GBA2
Accounts and Accounting Reference Dates	GBA3
Auditors	GBA4
Late Filing Penalties	GBA5
Share Capital and Prospectuses	GBA6
Resolutions	GBA7
Company Charges and Mortgages	GBA8
Company Charges (Scotland)	GBA8(S)
Flat Management Companies	GBA9
Dormant Companies	GBA10

Winding up

Liquidation and Insolvency	GBW1
Liquidation and Insolvency (Scotland)	GBW1(S)
Strike-off, Dissolution and Restoration	GBW2
Strike-off, Dissolution and Restoration (Scotland)	GBW2(S)

Other

Oversea Companies	GBO11
Limited Partnership Act	GBO2
Newspaper Libel and Registration Act	GBO3
European Economic Interest Groupings	GNBO4
Use of Welsh	GBF1

appendix D

**Examples of completed
Companies House forms**

The forms in this appendix are among those most likely to be of interest to company secretaries. In order to illustrate the principles, they have been completed to show events in fictitious companies. The forms included in this appendix are as follows:

Form number	Form title
10 (4 pages)	First directors and secretary and situation of registered office
12	Declaration on application for registration
88(2) (2 pages)	Return of allotment of Shares
117 (2 pages)	Application by a public company for certificate to commence business
123	Notice of increase in nominal capital
169	Return by a company purchasing its own shares
225	Change of accounting reference date
287	Change in situation or address of registered office
288a (2 pages)	Appointment of Director/Secretary
288b	Terminating appointment as director
288c	Change of particulars for director or secretary
353	Register of members
391	Notice of passing of resolution removing an auditor
395 (2 pages)	Particulars of a mortgage or charge
403a	Declaration of satisfaction in full or in part of mortgage or charge
405(1)	Notice of appointment of receiver or manager
652a	Application for striking off

10

Companies House
— for the record —

Please complete in typescript,
or in bold black capitals.
CHFP000

Notes on completion appear on final page

First directors and secretary and intended situation of registered office

Company Name in full | Dolblatt Ltd

Proposed Registered Office | 34 Basin Street

(PO Box numbers only, are not acceptable)

Post town | Kettering

County / Region | Northamptonshire | Postcode | NN14 4LL

If the memorandum is delivered by an agent for the subscriber(s) of the memorandum mark the box opposite and give the agent's name and address.

Agent's Name

Address

SPECIMEN

Post town

County / Region | Postcode

Number of continuation sheets attached | 0

You do not have to give any contact information in the box opposite but if you do, it will help Companies House to contact you if there is a query on the form. The contact information that you give will be visible to searchers of the public record.

Mrs J K Smith, 18 Hill Avenue, Kettering
Northamptonshire NN14 9KT
Tel 01536 429471
DX number | DX exchange

Companies House receipt date barcode
This form is been provided free of charge by Companies House

Form April 2002

When you have completed and signed the form please send it to the Registrar of Companies at:
Companies House, Crown Way, Cardiff, CF14 3UZ | **DX 33050 Cardiff**
for companies registered in England and Wales
or
Companies House, 37 Castle Terrace, Edinburgh, EH1 2EB
for companies registered in Scotland | **DX 235 Edinburgh**

Company Secretary (see notes 1-5)

Company name	Dolblatt Limited

NAME *Style / Title: Mrs   *Honours etc:

* Voluntary details

Forename(s): Julia Kate

Surname: Smith

Previous forename(s):

Previous surname(s):

†† Tick this box if the address shown is a service address for the beneficiary of a Confidentiality Order granted under section 723B of the Companies Act 1985 otherwise, give your usual residential address. In the case of a corporation or Scottish firm, give the registered or principal office address.

Address ††: 18 Hill Avenue

Post town: Kettering

County / Region: Northamptonshire   Postcode: NN14 9KT

Country: England

I consent to act as secretary of the company named on page 1

Consent: *Julia Smith*   **Date** 1st April 2003

Directors (see notes 1-5)

Please list directors in alphabetical order

NAME *Style / Title: Sir   *Honours etc: CBE

Forename(s): William Peter

Surname: Crown

Previous forename(s):

Previous surname(s):

†† Tick this box if the address shown is a service address for the beneficiary of a Confidentiality Order granted under section 723B of the Companies Act 1985 otherwise, give your usual residential address. In the case of a corporation or Scottish firm, give the registered or principal office address.

Address ††: 14 Larch Avenue

Post town: Kingston-upon-Thames

County / Region: Surrey   Postcode: KT3 2RB

Country: England

Date of birth: Day 1 7 Month 0 3 Year 1 9 4 4   **Nationality** British

Business occupation: Civil Engineer

Other directorships: Javata Holdings Limited

I consent to act as director of the company named on page 1

Consent signature: *W. P. Crown*   **Date** 1st April 2003

SPECIMEN

Directors (see notes 1-5)

Please list directors in alphabetical order

NAME *Style / Title* | Mr | *Honours etc* |

Forename(s) | Kevin

Surname | Thomas

Previous forename(s) | Arthur

Previous surname(s) |

† Tick this box if the address shown is a service address for the beneficiary of a Confidentiality Order granted under section 723B of the Companies Act 1985 otherwise, give your usual residential address. In the case of a corporation or Scottish firm, give the registered or principal office address.

Address † | 79 Riverside Walk

Post town | Kingston-upon-Thames

County / Region | Surrey | Postcode | KT4 6PN

Country | England

Date of birth | Day 2 4 | Month 1 1 | Year 1 | Nationality | Australian

Business occupation | Civil Engineer

Other directorships |

SPECIMEN

I consent to act as director of the company named on page 1

Consent signature | K. Thomas | Date | 1st April 2003

This section must be signed by
Either

an agent on behalf of all subscribers | Signed | | Date |

Or the subscribers | Signed | W. P. Crown | Date | 1st April 2003

(i.e those who signed as members on the memorandum of association). | Signed | L. L. Crown | Date | 1st April 2003

Signed | Keith Bradshaw | Date | 1st April 2003

Signed | T. T. R. O'Reilley | Date | 1st April 2003

Signed | | Date |

Signed | | Date |

Notes

1. Show for an individual the full forename(s) NOT INITIALS and surname together with any previous forename(s) or surname(s).

If the director or secretary is a corporation or Scottish firm - show the corporate or firm name on the surname line.

Give previous forename(s) or surname(s) except that:

- for a married woman, the name by which she was known before marriage need not be given,

- names not used since the age of 18 or for at least 20 years need not be given.

A peer, or an individual known by a title, may state the title instead of or in addition to the forename(s) and surname and need not give the name by which that person was known before he or she adopted the title or succeeded to it.

Address:

Give the usual residential address.

In the case of a corporation or Scottish firm give the registered or principal office.

Subscribers:

The form must be signed personally either by the subscriber(s) or by a person or persons authorised to sign on behalf of the subscriber(s).

2. Directors known by another description:

- A director includes any person who occupies that position even if called by a different name, for example, governor, member of council.

3. Directors details:

- Show for each individual director the director's date of birth, business occupation and nationality. **The date of birth must be given for every individual director.**

4. Other directorships:

- Give the name of every company of which the person concerned is a director or has been a director at any time in the past 5 years. You may exclude a company which either **is** or at **all times during the past 5 years,** when the person was a director, was:

- dorm...

- a parent company which wholly owned the company making the return,

- a wholly owned subsidiary of the company making the return, or

- another wholly owned subsidiary of the same parent company.

If there is insufficient space on the form for other directorships you may use a separate sheet of paper, which should include the company's number and the full name of the director.

5. Use Form 10 continuation sheets or photocopies of page 2 to provide details of joint secretaries or additional directors.

SPECIMEN

FORM 12

SPECIMEN

Companies House
—— *for the record* ——

*Please complete in typescript,
or in bold black capitals.*

CHFP000

(NCPack)

12

Declaration on application for registration

Company Name in full	Dolblatt Limited
I,	Sir William Peter Crown
of	44 Larch Avenue, Kingston-upon-Thames KT3 2RB

do solemnly and sincerely declare that I am a † [Solicitor engaged in the formation of the company][person named as director or secretary of the company in the statement delivered to the Registrar under section 10 of the Companies Act 1985] and that all the requirements of the Companies Act 1985 in respect of the registration of the above company and of matters precedent and incidental to it have been complied with.

† Please delete as appropriate.

And I make this solemn Declaration conscientiously believing the same to be true and by virtue of the Statutory Declarations Act 1835.

Declarant's signature

Declared at

	Day	Month	Year
On			

❶ Please print name.

before me **❶**

Signed		**Date**	

† A Commissioner for Oaths or Notary Public or Justice of the Peace or Solicitor

Please give the name, address, telephone number and, if available, a DX number and Exchange of the person Companies House should contact if there is any query.

Mrs J K Smith, 18 Hill Avenue, Kettering,
Northamptonshire NN14 9KT
Tel 01536 429471
DX number   DX exchange

Companies House receipt date barcode

This form has been provided free of charge by Companies House.

Form revised June 1998

When you have completed and signed the form please send it to the Registrar of Companies at:
Companies House, Crown Way, Cardiff, CF14 3UZ   DX 33050 Cardiff
for companies registered in England and Wales
or
Companies House, 37 Castle Terrace, Edinburgh, EH1 2EB
for companies registered in Scotland   **DX 235 Edinburgh**

THE FIRST PAGE OF FORM 88(2)

Companies House
—— *for the record* ——

88(2)

Return of Allotment of Shares

Please complete in typescript, or in bold black capitals.

CHFP000

Company Number

1843666

Company name in full

Dolblatt Limited

Shares allotted (including bonus shares):

	From			To		
	Day	Month	Year	Day	Month	Year

Date or period during which shares were allotted
(If shares were allotted on one date enter that date in the "from" box)

From: 1 8 | 0 4 | 2 0 0 3

Class of shares *(ordinary or preference etc)*	Preference		
Number allotted	100,000		
Nominal value of each share	£1.00		
Amount (if any) paid or due on each share *(including any share premium)*	£1.00		

List the names and addresses of the allottees and the number of shares allotted to each overleaf

If the allotted shares are fully or partly paid up otherwise than in cash please state:

% that each share is to be treated as paid up			

Consideration for which the shares were allotted
(This information must be supported by the duly stamped contract or by the duly stamped particulars on Form 88(3) if the contract is not in writing)

Companies House receipt date barcode

This form has been provided free of charge by Companies House.

Form revised January 2000

When you have completed and signed the form send it to the Registrar of Companies at:

Companies House, Crown Way, Cardiff CF14 3UZ   **DX 33050 Cardiff**
For companies registered in England and Wales

Companies House, 37 Castle Terrace, Edinburgh EH1 2EB   **DX 235**
For companies registered in Scotland   **Edinburgh**

THE SECOND PAGE OF FORM 88(2)

Names and addresses of the allottees *(List joint share allotments consecutively)*

Shareholder details	Class of shares allotted	Number allotted
Name J T Investments Limited **Address** 36 Kingfisher Street London UK Postcode E C 4 R 2 9 V	Preference	33,334
Name Claud Charles Green **Address** The Poplars, Warwick Avenue Coventry UK Postcode C V 4 7 R T	Preference	33,333
Name Marjorie Dawn Green **Address** The Poplars, Warwick Avenue Coventry UK Postcode C V 4 7 R T	Preference	33,333
Name **Address** UK Postcode		
Name **Address** UK Postcode		

SPECIMEN

Please enter the number of continuation sheets (if any) attached to this form

Signed *Julia Smith*　　　　**Date** 18th April 2003

A director / secretary / ~~administrator / administrative receiver / receiver manager / receiver~~　　*Please delete as appropriate*

Please give the name, address, telephone number and, if available, a DX number and Exchange of the person Companies House should contact if there is any query.

Mrs J K Smith, 18 Hill Avenue, Kettering, Northamptonshire NN14 9KT

Tel 01536 429471

DX number	DX exchange

THE FIRST PAGE OF FORM 117

Companies House
— for the record —

Please complete in typescript,
or in bold black capitals.

CHFP000

117

Application by a public company for certificate to commence business

Company Number | 1847223

Company Name in full | Hemel Construction PLC

applies for a certificate that it is entitled to do business and exercise borrowing powers, and, for that purpose,

I, | Gordon Michael Fraser

of | Hemel Construction PLC, Park House, Park
Street, Hemel Hempstread, Hertfordshire HP20 4DD

❶ Please delete as appropriate.

❶ [a director][the secretary] of the above company do solemnly and sincerely declare that:-

1. the aggregate nominal value of the company's allotted share capital is not less than £...

2. the aggregate amount paid up on the allotted share capital of the company at the time of this application is | £ 1,000,000

3. the ❶ [estimated] amount of the preliminary expenses of the company is | £ 30,000

❷ Please insert the name(s) of person(s) by whom expenses paid or payable.

❷ Margaret Brown

Hemel Construction PLC

Park House, Park Street

Hemel Hempstead

Hertfordshire HP20 4DD

Please give the name, address, telephone number and, if available, a DX number and Exchange of the person Companies House should contact if there is any query.

G M Fraser, Hemel Construction PLC

Park House, Park Street, Hemel Hempstead,

Herts HP20 4DD   Tel 01442 656518

DX number   DX exchange

Companies House receipt date barcode

This form has been provided free of charge by Companies House.

Form revised July 1998

When you have completed and signed the form please send it to the Registrar of Companies at:
Companies House, Crown Way, Cardiff, CF14 3UZ   DX 33050 Cardiff
for companies registered in England and Wales
or
Companies House, 37 Castle Terrace, Edinburgh, EH1 2EB
for companies registered in Scotland   **DX 235 Edinburgh**

SPECIMEN

❶[4a. no amount or benefit has been paid or given or is intended to be paid or given to any of the promoters of the company]

❶[4b. the amount or benefit paid or given or intended to be paid or given to any promoter of the company is:]

❶ Please delete as appropriate.

Promoter No 1;

The amount paid or intended to be paid	£
Any benefit given or intended to be given	
The consideration for such payment or benefit	

Promoter No 2;

The amount paid or intended to be paid	£
Any benefit given or intended to be given	
The consideration for such payment or benefit	

Promoter No 3;

The amount paid or intended to be paid	£
Any benefit given or intended to be given	
The consideration for such payment or benefit	

And I make this solemn Declaration conscientiously believing the same to be true and by virtue of the Statutory Declarations Act 1835.

Declarant's signature

Declared at

	Day	Month	Year
on			

❷Please print name.

before me ❸

Signed _____ **Date** _____

A Commissioner for Oaths or Notary Public or Justice of the Peace or Solicitor

G

COMPANIES FORM No. 123

Notice of increase in nominal capital

123

CHFP000

Please do not write in this margin

Pursuant to section 123 of the Companies Act 1985

Please complete legibly, preferably in black type, or bold block lettering

To the Registrar of Companies
(Address overleaf)

For official use

Company number
13112174

* insert full name of company

Name of company

.Anglian Garden Accessories Limited

gives notice in accordance with section 123 of the above Act that by resolution of the company

dated 28th March 2003 _____ the nominal capital of the company has been

increased by £ 200,000 _____ beyond the registered capital of £ 300,000 _____ .

† the copy must be printed or in some other form approved by the registrar

A copy of the resolution authorising the increase is attached. †

The conditions (eg. voting rights, dividend rights, winding-up rights etc.) subject to which the new

shares have been or are to be issued are as follows :

The conditions are in all respects identical to the conditions
of the existing shares in issue.

SPECIMEN

Please tick here if continued overleaf

‡ Insert Director, Secretary, Administrator, Administrative Receiver or Receiver (Scotland) as appropriate

Signed *T. L. Herbert*   Designation ‡ Secretary   Date 28th March 200

Presentor's name address and reference (if any) :
T L Herbert
14 Cathedral Street
Norwich
NR2 6RT

For official Use   (02/00)
General Section

Post room

FORM 169

G

CHFP000

COMPANIES FORM No. 169

Return by a company purchasing its own shares

169

Pursuant to section 169 of the Companies Act 1985

Please do not write in this margin

Please complete legibly, preferably in black type, or bold block lettering

To the Registrar of Companies **(Address overleaf)**

For official use

Company number

1429923

Please do not write in the space below. For Inland Revenue use only.

Name of company

* insert full name of company

* Klaus Barometers Limited

Note
This return must be delivered to the Registrar within a period of 28 days beginning with the first date on which shares to which it relates were delivered to the company

Shares were purchased by the company under section 162 of the above Act as follows:

Class of shares	Ordinary		
Number of shares purchased	500,000		
Nominal value of each share	20p		
Date(s) on which the shares were delivered to the company	10th April 2003		
Maximum prices paid § for each share	60p		
Minimum prices paid § for each share	60p		

§ A private company is not required to give this information

SPECIMEN

The aggregate amount paid by the company for the shares to which this return relates was:	£ 300,000
Stamp duty payable pursuant to section 66 of the Finance Act 1986 on the aggregate amount at 50p per £100 or part of £100	£ 1,500

‡ Insert Director, Secretary, Administrator, Administrative Receiver or Receiver (Scotland) as appropriate

Signed _T. Klaus_   Designation ‡ Secretary   Date 16th April 200

Presentor's name address and reference (if any) :
T Klaus
Klaus Barometers
Limited
421 Coventry Road
Birmingham
B8 9EH

For official Use
General Section

Post room

261

FORM 225

Companies House
— *for the record* —

Please complete in typescript, or in bold black capitals
CHFP000

225

Change of accounting reference date

Company Number	1511628

Company Name in Full	Plymouth Textiles Limited

NOTES
You may use this form to change the accounting date relating to either the current or the immediately previous accounting period.

a. You **may not** change a period for which the accounts are already overdue.

b. You **may not** extend a period beyond 18 months unless the company is subject to an administration order.

c. You **may not** extend periods more than once in five years unless:

1. the company is subject to an administration order, or

2. you have the specific approval of the Secretary of State, (please enclose a copy), or

3. you are extending the company's accounting reference period to align with that of a parent or subsidiary undertaking established in the European Economic Area, or

4. the form is being submitted by an oversea company.

	Day	Month	Year
The accounting reference period ending	3 1	0 3	2 0 0 3

	Day	Month	Year
is shortened/extended† so as to end on	3 0	0 4	2 0 0 3

Subsequent periods will end on the same day and month in future years.

If extending more than once in five years, please indicate in the box the number of the provision listed in note c. on which you are relying.

Signed	*L. Trapp*	Date	26th February 2003

† Please delete as appropriate

~~† a director / secretary / administrator / administrative receiver / receiver and manager / receiver (Scotland) / person authorised on behalf of an oversea company~~

Please give the name, address, telephone number, and if available, a DX number and Exchange, for the person Companies House should contact if there is any query

Mrs L Trapp, Plymouth Textiles Limited
48 Drake Terrace, Plymouth, Devon PL2 9RY
Tel 01752 666114

DX number	DX exchange

Companies House receipt date barcode

This form has been provided free of charge by Companies House.

Form revised July 1998

When you have completed and signed the form please send it to the Registrar of Companies at:

Companies House, Crown Way, Cardiff, CF14 3UZ   DX 33050 Cardiff
for companies registered in England and Wales

or

Companies House, 37 Castle Terrace, Edinburgh, EH1 2EB
for companies registered in Scotland   **DX 235 Edinburgh**

FORM 287

Companies House
— for the record —

287

Please complete in typescript,
or in bold black capitals.
CHFP000

Change in situation or address of Registered Office

Company Number	151.1628
Company Name in full	Plymouth Textiles Limited

New situation of registered office

NOTE:

The change in the situation of the registered office does not take effect until the Registrar has registered this notice.

For 14 days beginning with the date that a change of registered office is registered, a person may validly serve any document on the company at its previous registered office.

PO Box numbers only are not acceptable.

Address	48 Drake Terrace
Post town	Plymouth
County / Region	Devonshire
Postcode	PL2 9RY

SPECIMEN

Signed	*L. Trapp*
Date	28th February 2003

† Please delete as appropriate.

† a director / secretary / ~~administrator / administrative receiver / liquidator / receiver manager / receiver~~

Please give the name, address, telephone number and, if available, a DX number and Exchange of the person Companies House should contact if there is any query.

Mrs L Trapp, Plymouth Textiles Limited
48 Drake Terrace, Plymouth, Devon PL2 9RY
Tel 01752 666114

DX number	DX exchange

Companies House receipt date barcode

This form has been provided free of charge by Companies House.

Form revised June 1998

When you have completed and signed the form please send it to the Registrar of Companies at:
Companies House, Crown Way, Cardiff, CF14 3UZ   **DX 33050 Cardiff**
for companies registered in England and Wales
or
Companies House, 37 Castle Terrace, Edinburgh, EH1 2EB
for companies registered in Scotland   **DX 235 Edinburgh**

Companies House
— for the record —

Please complete in typescript, or in bold black capitals.

CHFP000

288a

APPOINTMENT of director or secretary
(NOT for resignation (use Form 288b) or change of particulars (use Form 288c))

Company Number | 151.1628

Company Name in full | Plymouth Textiles Limited

	Day	Month	Year			Day	Month	Year
Date of appointment	3 1	0 3	2 0 0 3	†Date of Birth		1 4	1 2	1 9 7 4

Appointment form

Notes on completion appear on reverse.

Appointment as director ☒ as secretary ☐

Please mark the appropriate box. If appointment is as a director and secretary mark both boxes.

NAME

*Style / Title | Miss

*Honours etc

Forename(s) | Sarah Jane

Surname | Blair

Previous Forename(s)

Previous Surname(s)

†† Tick this box if the address shown is a service address for the beneficiary of a Confidentiality Order granted under the provisions of section 723B of the Companies Act 1985

†† **Usual residential address** | ____, 33 Station Road

Post town | Exeter | Postcode | EX8 9RB

County / Region | Devonshire | Country | England

†Nationality | British | †Business occupation | Accountant

†Other directorships (additional space overleaf) | West Country Designs Limited

I consent to act as ** director / ~~secretary~~ of the above named company

Consent signature | *Sarah Blair* | **Date** 31st March 2003

* Voluntary details.
† Directors only.
**Delete as appropriate

A director, secretary etc must sign the form below.

Signed | *L. Trapp* | **Date** 31st March 2003

(**a ~~director~~ / secretary / ~~administrator / administrative receiver / receiver manager / receiver~~)

You do not have to give any contact information in the box opposite but if you do, it will help Companies House to contact you if there is a query on the form. The contact information that you give will be visible to searchers of the public record..

Mrs L Trapp, Plymouth Textiles Limited

48 Drake Terrace, Plymouth, Devonshire

PL2 9RY | Tel 01752 666114

DX number | DX exchange

Companies House receipt date barcode

This form has been provided free of charge by Companies House

When you have completed and signed the form please send it to the Registrar of Companies at:

Companies House, Crown Way, Cardiff, CF14 3UZ   **DX 33050 Cardiff**
for companies registered in England and Wales   **or**
Companies House, 37 Castle Terrace, Edinburgh, EH1 2EB
for companies registered in Scotland   **DX 235 Edinburgh**

Form April 2002

SPECIMEN

Company Number

† Directors only.

†Other directorships

NOTES

Show the full forenames, NOT INITIALS. If the director or secretary is a corporation or Scottish firm, show the name on surname line and registered or principal office on the usual residential line.

Give previous forenames or surname(s) except:
- for a married woman, the name by which she was known before marriage need not be given.
- for names not used since the age of 18 or for at least 20 years

A peer or individual known by a title may state the title instead of or in addition to the forenames and surname and need not give the name by which that person was known before he or she adopted the title or succeeded to it.

Other directorships.

Give the name of every company incorporated in Great Britain of which the person concerned is a director or has been a director at any time in the past five years.

You may exclude a company which either is, or at all times during the past five years when the person concerned was a director, was
- dormant
- a parent company which wholly owned the company making the return, or
- another wholly owned subsidiary of the same parent company.

FORM 288B

Please complete in typescript,
or in bold black capitals.
CHFP000

288b

Terminating appointment as director or secretary
(NOT for appointment (use Form 288a) or change of particulars (use Form 288c))

Company Number | 1511628

Company Name in full | Plymouth Textiles Limited

Date of termination of appointment

Day	Month	Year
1 0	0 4	2 0 0 3

as director ☐   as secretary ☐

Please mark the appropriate box. If terminating appointment as a director and secretary mark both boxes.

NAME

Please insert details as previously notified to Companies House.

*Style / Title | Mr
*Honours etc |

Forename(s) | Cedric Malcolm

Surname | Richardson

Day	Month	Year
†Date of Birth | 1 3 | 0 8 | 1 9 4 2 |

SPECIMEN

A serving director, secretary etc must sign the form below.

Signed | *L. Trapp*   **Date** | 10th April 2003

* Voluntary details.
† Directors only.
** Delete as appropriate

(** serving ~~director~~ / secretary / ~~administrator~~ / ~~administrative receiver~~ / ~~receiver manager~~ / ~~receiver~~)

Please give the name, address, telephone number and, if available, a DX number and Exchange of the person Companies House should contact if there is any query.

Mrs L Trapp, Plymouth Textiles Limited

48 Drake Terrace, Plymouth, Devon PL2 9RY

Tel 01752 666114

DX number | DX exchange

When you have completed and signed the form please send it to the Registrar of Companies at:
Companies House, Crown Way, Cardiff, CF14 3UZ   DX 33050 Cardiff
for companies registered in England and Wales   **or**
Companies House, 37 Castle Terrace, Edinburgh, EH1 2EB
for companies registered in Scotland   **DX 235 Edinburgh**

Companies House receipt date barcode

This form has been provided free of charge by Companies House.

Form revised 1999

266

FORM 288C

Companies House
for the record

*Please complete in typescript,
or in bold black capitals.*

CHWP000

288c

CHANGE OF PARTICULARS for director
or secretary *(NOT for appointment (use Form*
288a) or resignation (use Form 288b))

Company Number	1511628
Company Name in full	Plymouth Textiles Limited

Changes of particulars form   *Complete in all cases*

	Day	Month	Year
Date of change of particulars	2 0	0 4	2 0 0 3

Name

*Style / Title	Miss	*Honours etc	
Forename(s)	Sarah Jane		
Surname	Blair		

	Day	Month	Year
† Date of Birth	1 4	1 2	1 9 7 4

Change of name *(enter new name)* Forename(s)

Surname

Change of usual residential address ††
(enter new address)

96 Oak...ge Avenue

†† Tick this box if the address shown is a service address for the beneficiary of a Confidentiality Order granted under the provisions of section 723B of the Companies Act 1985 ☒

Post town	Exeter		
County / Region	Devonshire	Postcode	EX8 4LT
Country	England		

Other change
(please specify)

A serving director, secretary etc must sign the form below.

* Voluntary details.
† Directors only.
**Delete as appropriate.

Signed *L. Trapp*   **Date** 20th April 2003

(** director / secretary / administrator / administrative receiver / receiver manager / receiver)

You do not have to give any contact information in the box opposite but if you do, it will help Companies House to contact you if there is a query on the form. The contact information that you give will be visible to searchers of the public record..

Mrs L Trapp, Plymouth Textiles Limited
48 Drake Terrace, Plymouth, Devonshire
PL2 9RY   Tel 01752 666114

DX number	DX exchange

Companies House receipt date barcode

This form has been provided free of charge by Companies House

Form April 2002

When you have completed and signed the form please send it to the Registrar of Companies at:
Companies House, Crown Way, Cardiff, CF14 3UZ   DX 33050 Cardiff
for companies registered in England and Wales   **or**
Companies House, 37 Castle Terrace, Edinburgh, EH1 2EB
for companies registered in Scotland   **DX 235 Edinburgh**

FORM 353

Companies House
— *for the record* —

Please complete in typescript,
or in bold black capitals.

CHFP000

Register of members

353

Company Number | 1511628

Company Name in full | Plymouth Textiles Limited

The register of members is kept at:

NOTE:

The register **MUST** be kept at an address in the country of incorporation.

This notice is not required where the register has, at all times since it came into existence (or in the case of a register in existence on 1 July 1948 at all times since then) been kept at the registered office.

Address | Blenkinsop and Pike (Solicitors)
| 16 Broad Drive

Post town | Plymouth

County / Region | Devonshire | **Postcode** | PL1 4RK

SPECIMEN

Signed | *L. Trapp* | **Date** | 20th April 2003

† Please delete as appropriate.

† a director / secretary / administrator / administrative receiver / receiver manager / receiver

Please give the name, address, telephone number and, if available, a DX number and Exchange of the person Companies House should contact if there is any query.

Mrs L Trapp, Plymouth Textiles Limited
48 Drake Terrace, Plymouth, Devonshire

PL2 9RY | Tel 01752 666114

DX number | DX exchange

Companies House receipt date barcode

Form revised March 1995

When you have completed and signed the form please send it to the Registrar of Companies at:

Companies House, Crown Way, Cardiff, CF4 3UZ | **DX 33050 Cardiff**
for companies registered in England and Wales
or
Companies House, 37 Castle Terrace, Edinburgh, EH1 2EB
for companies registered in Scotland | **DX 235 Edinburgh**

FORM 391

Companies House
for the record

Please complete in typescript,
or in bold black capitals.
CHFP000

391

Notice of passing of resolution removing an auditor

Company Number	1511628
Company Name in full	Plymouth Textiles Limited

Date of resolution

Day	Month	Year
2 0	0 4	2 0 0 3

Date of removal

Day	Month	Year
3 0	0 4	2 0 0 3

Details of auditor removed from office   Clancy and Brown

Firm / Partnership / Individual   Partnership

Address   Abacus House

Cliff Street

Post town   Saltash

County / Region   Devonshire   **Postcode** PL22 3BC

SPECIMEN

Signed   L. Trapp   **Date**   20th April 2003

† Please delete as appropriate.

† a director / secretary

Please give the name, address, telephone number and, if available, a DX number and Exchange of the person Companies House should contact if there is any query.

Mrs L Trapp, Plymouth Textiles Limited

48 Drake Terrace, Plymouth, Devonshire

PL2 2RY   **Tel** 01752 666114

DX number   DX exchange

Companies House receipt date barcode

This form has been provided free of charge by Companies House.

Form revised July 1998

When you have completed and signed the form please send it to the Registrar of Companies at:

Companies House, Crown Way, Cardiff, CF14 3UZ   **DX 33050 Cardiff**
for companies registered in England and Wales
or
Companies House, 37 Castle Terrace, Edinburgh, EH1 2EB
for companies registered in Scotland   **DX 235 Edinburgh**

M

COMPANIES FORM No. 395

Particulars of a mortgage or charge

395

Pursuant to section 395 of the Companies Act 1985

Please do not
write in
this margin

*Please complete
legibly, preferably
in black type, or
bold block lettering*

To the Registrar of Companies
(Address overleaf - Note 5)

For official use

Company number

1511628

Name of company

* insert full name
of Company

* Plymouth Textiles Limited

Date of creation of the charge

21st April 2003

Description of the instrument (if any) creating or evidencing the charge (note 2)

Legal charge

Amount secured by the mortgage or charge

£100,000 (one hundred thousand pounds only)

Names and addresses of the mortgagees or persons entitled to the charge

Barletts Bank PLC, 44 Cheapside, London

Postcode | EC4P 3LR

Presentor's name address and
reference (if any) :
Mrs L Trapp
Plymouth Textiles
Limited
48 Drake Terrace
Plymouth PL2 9RY

For official Use
Mortgage Section

Post room

Time critical reference

Page 1

Short particulars of all the property mortgaged or charged

The freehold property comprising 48 Drake Terrace, Plymouth
Devonshire PL2 9RY (Title Number DE45768)

Please do not
write in
this margin

*Please complete
legibly, preferably
in black type, or
bold block lettering*

Particulars as to commission allowance or discount (note 3)

NIL

Signed   L. Trapp   Date 24th April 2003

On behalf of [company][mortgagee/chargee]†   † delete as
appropriate

Notes

1 The original instrument (if any) creating or evidencing the charge, together with these prescribed
   particulars correctly completed must be delivered to the Registrar of Companies within 21 days
   after the date of creation of the charge (section 395). If the property is situated and the charge was
   created outside the United Kingdom delivery to the Registrar must be effected within 21 days after
   the date on which the instrument could in due course of post, and if dispatched with due diligence,
   have been received in the United Kingdom (section 398). A copy of the instrument creating the
   charge will be accepted where the property charged is situated and the charge was created outside
   the United Kingdom (section 398) and in such cases the copy must be verified to be a correct copy
   either by the company or by the person who has delivered or sent the copy to the registrar. The
   verification must be signed by or on behalf of the person giving the verification and where this is
   given by a body corporate it must be signed by an officer of that body. A verified copy will also be
   accepted where section 398(4) applies (property situate in Scotland or Northern Ireland) and Form
   No. 398 is submitted.

2 A description of the instrument, eg "Trust Deed", "Debenture", "Mortgage", or "Legal charge", etc, as
   the case may be, should be given.

3 In this section there should be inserted the amount or rate per cent. of the commission, allowance
   or discount (if any) paid or made either directly or indirectly by the company to any person in
   consideration of his:
       (a) subscribing or agreeing to subscribe, whether absolutely or conditionally, or
       (b) procuring or agreeing to procure subscriptions, whether absolute or conditional,
   for any of the debentures included in this return. The rate of interest payable under the terms of the
   debentures should not be entered.

4 If any of the spaces in this form provide insufficient space the particulars must be entered on the
   prescribed continuation sheet.

5 The address of the Registrar of Companies is:-

Companies House, Crown Way, Cardiff CF4 3UZ   Page 2

SPECIMEN

FORM 403A

M

CHFP000

COMPANIES FORM No. 403a

Declaration of satisfaction in full or in part of mortgage or charge

403a

Please do not write in this margin

Pursuant to section 403(1) of the Companies Act 1985

Please complete legibly, preferably in black type, or bold block lettering

To the Registrar of Companies **(Address overleaf)**

Name of company

For official use

Company number
1511628

* insert full name of company

* Plymouth Textiles Limited .

I, Linda Trapp

of 48 Drake Terrace, Plymouth, Devonshire PL2 9RY

† delete as appropriate

[a director][the secretary][the administrator][the administrative receiver]† of the above company, do solemnly and sincerely declare that the debt for which the charge described below was given has been paid or satisfied in [full][part]†

insert a description of the instrument(s) creating or evidencing the charge, eg 'Mortgage', 'Charge', 'Debenture' etc

Date and description of charge # Legal charge dated on 21st April 2003

Date of registration ø _____ 24th April

ø the date of registration may be confirmed from the certificate

Name and address of [chargee][trustee for the debenture holders]† Bartletts Bank PLC, 44 Cheapside, London EC4 3LX

§ insert brief details of property

Short particulars of property charged § ... freehold property comprising 48 Drake Terrace, Plymouth, Devonshire PL2 9RY

And I make this solemn declaration conscientiously believing the same to be true and by virtue of the provisions of the Statutory Declarations Act 1835.

Declared at _____

Declarant to sign below

_____

	Day	Month	Year
on			

before me _____

A Commissioner for Oaths or Notary Public or Justice of the Peace or a Solicitor having the powers conferred on a Commissioner for Oaths.

Presenter's name address and reference (if any) :
Mrs L Trapp
Plymouth Textiles
Limited
48 Drake Terrace
Plymouth, Devonshire
PL2 9RY

For official Use (02/00)
Mortgage Section

Post room

SPECIMEN

272

M

COMPANIES FORM No.405(1)

Notice of appointment of receiver or manager

Pursuant to section 405(1) of the Companies Act 1985

405(1)

Please do not write in this binding margin

Please complete legibly, preferably in black type, or bold block lettering

* insert full name of company

ø insert name and address of receiver/manager

† delete as appropriate

§ name of court making the order

‡ enter description and date of the instrument under which appointment is made, and state whether it is a debenture secured by a floating charge

To the Registrar of Companies (Address overleaf)

For official use

Company number

1398878

Name of company

* Abley Stationery Limited

I/We Robert Simon Cabot

of Cabot House, Clay Street, Weston-Super-Mare, Avon BS23 4NN

give notice that

ø Mrs Pauline White of Jones and White (Chartered Accountants), 49 King Street, Bristol BS8 1VN

was appointed as [receiver][manager][receiver-and-manager][manager] the property of the company.

The appointment was made by

[an order of the § High Court

made on 28th March 2003]†

[me/us on 17th August 1992 under the powers contained in‡ a debenture secured by a floating charge

]†

SPECIMEN

Signed Robert S. Cabot

Date 28th March 2003

Presentor's name address and reference (if any):
Mr R S Cabot
Cabot Stationery
Limited
Cabot House
Clay Street
Weston-Super-Mare
Avon BS23 4NN

For official Use
Liquidation Section

Post room

Time critical reference

FORM 652A

Companies House
—— *for the record* ——

Please complete in typescript, or in bold black capitals

CHFP000

652a

Application for striking off

Company Number	1422733
Company Name In Full	Abartley Limited

I/We as **DIRECTOR(S)** apply for this company to be struck off the register.

In the past three months the company has not:

- traded or otherwise carried on business, or changed its name;

- disposed of for value any property or rights which it would have disposed of for value in the normal course of trading or carrying on business; or

- engaged in any other activity except for the purpose of making this application, settling its debts or meeting a statutory requirement.

This company is not the subject of, nor the proposed subject of, insolvency proceedings or a section 425 scheme.

I/We enclose the fee of £10 (made payable to Companies House).

Director signatures (use continuation sheet if necessary).

WARNING: TO ALL APPLICANTS

IT IS AN OFFENCE KNOWINGLY OR RECKLESSLY TO PROVIDE FALSE OR MISLEADING INFORMATION ON THIS APPLICATION. YOU ARE ADVISED TO READ THE NOTES OVERLEAF AND TO CONSULT THE GUIDANCE NOTES AVAILABLE FROM COMPANIES HOUSE BEFORE COMPLETING THIS FORM. IF IN DOUBT, SEEK PROFESSIONAL ADVICE.

WARNING: TO ALL INTERESTED PARTIES.

THIS IS AN IMPORTANT NOTICE AND SHOULD NOT BE IGNORED. THE COMPANY NAMED HAS APPLIED TO THE REGISTRAR TO BE STRUCK OFF THE REGISTER AND DISSOLVED. ON DISSOLUTION ANY REMAINING ASSETS WILL PASS TO THE CROWN. THE REGISTRAR WILL STRIKE THE COMPANY OFF THE REGISTER UNLESS HE HAS REASONABLE CAUSE NOT TO DO SO. GUIDANCE NOTES ARE AVAILABLE ON GROUNDS FOR OBJECTION. IF IN DOUBT, SEEK PROFESSIONAL ADVICE.

Name of Director	William John Russell	
Signed	*W. J. Russell*	Date 3rd April 2003
Name of Director	Maria June Colville	
Signed	*Maria J. Colville*	Date 3rd April 2003
Name of Director		
Signed		Date

Please give the name, address, telephone number, and if available, a DX number and Exchange of the person Companies House should contact in connection with this application

Mr W J Russell, 43 Chiltern Avenue, Abingdon, Oxfordshire OX6 3LF

Tel 01235 414141

DX number	DX exchange

Companies House receipt date barcode

This form has been provided free of charge by Companies House.

Form revised July 1998

When you have signed the form send it with the fee to the Registrar of Companies at:

Companies House, Crown Way, Cardiff, CF14 3UZ   **DX 33050 Cardiff**
for companies registered in England and Wales
or
Companies House, 37 Castle Terrace Edinburgh, EH1 2EB
for companies registered in Scotland   **DX 235 Edinburgh**

appendix E

Full list of Companies House forms

Section A: General forms

Section B: Foreign forms

Section C: European economic interest
grouping forms

Section D: Disqualification forms

Section E: Limited partnership forms

Section F: Welsh bilingual forms

Section G: Investment company with variable
capital forms

Section H: Limited Liability partnership forms

Section I: Other forms available

Section A: General forms

Form No.	Description
6	Cancellation of alteration to the objects of a company
10	First directors and secretary and intended situation of registered office
10 cont	Continuation sheet to Form 10
12	Declaration on application for registration
30(5)(A)	Declaration on application for registration of a company exempt from the requirement to use the word "Limited" or "Cyfyngedig"
30(5)(B)	Declaration on application for registration under Section 680 of the CA 1985 of a company exempt from the requirement to use the word "Limited" or "Cyfyngedig"
30(5)(C)	Change of name omitting "Limited" or "Cyfyngedig"
43(3)	Application by a private company for re-registration as a public company
43(3)(E)	Declaration on application by a private company for re-registration as a public company
49(1)	Application by a limited company to be re-registered as unlimited
49(1) cont	Continuation sheet Form 49(1)
49(8)(A)	Members' assent to company being re-registered as unlimited
49(8)(A) cont	Members' assent to company being re-registered as unlimited (continuation)
49(8)(B)	Form of Statutory Declaration by directors as to members' assent to re-registration of a company as unlimited
51	Application by an unlimited company to be re-registered as limited

53	Application by a public company for re-registration as a private company
54	Application to the court for cancellation of resolution for re-registration
88(2)	Return of allotments of Shares
88(3)	Particulars of a contract relating to shares allotted as fully or partly paid up otherwise than in cash
97	Statement of the amount or rate per cent of any commission payable in connection with the subscription of shares
117	Application by a public company for certificate to commence business
122	Notice of consolidation, division, sub-division, redemption or cancellation of shares, or conversion, re-conversion of stock into shares
123	Notice of increase in nominal capital`
128(1)	Statement of rights attached to allotted shares
128(3)	Statement of particulars of variation of rights attached to shares
128(4)	Notice of assignment of name or new name of any class of shares
129(1)	Statement by a company without share capital of rights attached to newly created class of members
129(2)	Statement by a company without share capital of particulars of a variation of members' class rights
129(3)	Notice by a company without share capital of assignment of a name or other designation to a class of members
139	Application by a public company for re-registration as a private company following a Court Order reducing capital

147	Application by a public company for re-registration as a private company following cancellation of shares and reduction of nominal value of issued capital
155(6)(A)	Declaration in relation to assistance for the acquisition of shares
155(6)(B)	Declaration by the directors of a holding company in relation to assistance for the acquisition of shares
157	Notice of application made to the Court for the cancellation of a special resolution regarding financial assistance for the acquisition of shares
169	Return by a company purchasing its own shares
173	Declaration in relation to the redemption or purchase of shares out of capital
176	Notice of application to the court for the cancellation of a resolution for the redemption or purchase of shares out of capital
190	Location of register of debenture holders
190a	Notice of place for inspection of a register of holders of debentures which is kept in a non-legible form, or of any change in that place
225	Change of accounting reference date
244	Notice of claim to extension of period allowed for laying and delivering accounts - oversea business or interests
266(1)	Notice of intention to carry on business as an investment company
266(3)	Notice that a company no longer wishes to be an investment company
287	Change in situation or address of registered office
288a	Appointment of Director/Secretary
288b	Terminating Appointment of Director/Secretary
288c	Change of particulars for director or secretary

318	Location of directors' service contracts
325	Location of register of directors' interests in shares etc
325a	Notice of place for inspection of a register of directors' interests in shares etc which is kept in a non-legible form, or of any change in that place
353	Register of members
353a	Notice of place for inspection of a register of members which is kept in a non-legible form, or any change in that place
362	Notice of place where an overseas branch register is kept, of any change in that place, or of discontinuance of any such register
362a	Notice of place for inspection of an overseas branch register which is kept in a non-legible form, or of any change in that place
363A	Annual Return
363A cont	Annual Return (Continuation)
363A Sch	List of past and present members
391	Notice of passing of resolution removing an auditor
395	Particulars of a mortgage or charge
395 cont	Particulars of a mortgage or charge (continuation)
397	Particulars for the registration of a charge to secure a series of debentures
397a	Particulars of an issue of secured debentures in a series
398	Certificate of registration in Scotland or Northern Ireland of a charge comprising property situate there
400	Particulars of a charge subject to which property has been acquired

403a	Declaration of satisfaction in full or in part of mortgage or charge
403b	Declaration that part of the property or undertaking charged (a) has been released from the charge; (b) no longer forms part of the company's property or undertaking
405(1)	Notice of appointment of receiver or manager
405(2)	Notice of ceasing to act as receiver or manager
419(a)	Application of registration of a memorandum of satisfaction in full or in part of a registered charge. AVAILABLE FROM CH EDINBURGH
429(4)	Notice of non-assenting shareholders
429 dec	Statutory Declaration relating to a Notice to non-assenting shareholders
430A	Notice to non-assenting shareholders
600	Notice of appointment of liquidator voluntary winding up (members or creditors)
600a	Notice of appointment of liquidator voluntary winding up (members or creditors)
652a	Application for striking off
652a cont	Application for striking off (continuation sheet)
652c	Withdrawal of application for striking off
680a	Application by joint stock company for registration under part XXII of the Companies Act 1985, and Declaration and related statements
680b	Application by a company which is not a joint stock company for registration under part XXII of the Companies Act 1985, and Declaration and related statements
684	Registration under part XXII of the Companies Act 1985 List of members - existing joint stock company

	685	Declaration on application by a joint stock company for registration as a public company
	686	Registration under part XXII of the Companies Act 1985 Statutory Declaration verifying list of members
	R7	Application by an old public company for re-registration as a public company
	R7a	Notice of application made to the court for the cancellation of a special resolution by an old public company not to be re-registered as a public company
	R8	Declaration by director or secretary on application by an old public company for re-registration as public company
	R9	Declaration by old public company that it does not meet the requirements for a public company
	NLR1	Initial Registration/Annual Return form for a Newspaper
	NLR2	Newspaper Libel and Registration Act
Section B: **Foreign forms**	691	Return and declaration delivered for registration of a place of business by an oversea company
	681(1)(a)	Return of alteration in the charter, statutes, etc, of an oversea company
	692(1)(b)	Return of alteration in the directors or secretary of an ovesea company or in their particulars
	692(1)(c)	Return of alteration in the names and addresses of persons resident in Great Britain authorised to accept service on behalf of an oversea company
	692(2)	Return of change in the corporate name of an oversea company

694(4)(a)	Statement of name, other than corporate name, under which an oversea company proposes to carry on business in Great Britain
694(4)(b)	Statement of name, other than corporate name, under which an oversea company proposes to carry on business in Great Britain in substitution for a name previously registered
695A(3)	Notice of closure of a branch of an oversea company
703P(1)	Return by an oversea company that the company is being wound up
703P(3)	Notice of appointment of a liquidator of an oversea company
703P(5)	Notice by a liquidator of an oversea company concerning the termination of liquidation of the company
703Q(1)	Return by an oversea company which becomes subject to insolvency proceedings, etc
703Q(2)	Return by an oversea company on cessation of insolvency proceedings, etc
BR1	Return delivered for registration of a branch of an oversea company
BR2	Return by an oversea company subject to branch registration of an alteration to constitutional documents
BR3	Return by an oversea company subject to branch registration, for alteration of company particulars
BR4	Return by an oversea company subject to branch registration of change of directors or secretary or of their particulars
BR5	Return by an oversea company subject to branch registration of change of address or other branch particulars

	BR6	Return of change of person authorised to accept service or to represent the branch of an oversea company or of any change in their particulars
	BR7	Return by an oversea company of the branch at which the constitutional documents of the company have been registered in substitution for previous branch
Section C: European economic interest grouping forms	EEIG1	Statement of name, official address, members, objects and duration for EEIG whose official address is in Great Britain
	EEIG2	Statement of name, establishment address in Great Britain and members of an EEIG whose official address is outside the UK
	EEIG1 & 2 cont	Statement of members (continuation)
	EEIG3	Notice of manager's particulars, and of termination of appointment where the official address of the EEIG is in Great Britain
	EEIG4	Notice of documents and particulars required to be filed
	EEIG5	Notice of setting up or closure of an establishment of an EEIG
	EEIG6	Statement of name other than registered name, under which an EEIG whose official address is outside Great Britain proposes to carry on business in Great Britain
	EEIG7	Statement of name, other than registered name, under which an EEIG whose official address is outside Great Britain proposes to carry on business in substitution for name previously approved

Section D: Disqualification forms

DO1	Disqualification order against an individual
DO2	Disqualification order against a body corporate
DO3	Grant of leave in relation to a disqualification order
DO4	Variation or cessation of a disqualification order

Section E: Limited partnership forms

LP5	Application for Registration of a Limited Partnership
LP6	Limited Partnership Statement

Section F: Welsh bilingual forms

10 cym	Cyfarwyddwyr cyntaf ac ysgrifennydd, ynghyd a darpar leoliad y swyddfa gofrestredig
12 cym	Datganiad wrth wneud cais am gofrestriad
30(5)(a) cym	Datganiad wrth wneud cais am gofrestu cwmni sydd wedi ei ryddhau rhag angen defnyddio'r gair "limited" neu "cyfyngedig"
30(5)(b) cym	Datganiad wrth wneud cais am gofrestru, o dan adran 680 o Ddeddf Cwmniau 1985, gwmni sydd wedi ei ryddhau rhag angen defnyddio'r gair "limited" neu "cyfyngedig"
30(5)(c) cym	Newid enw, gan hepgor y gair "limited" neu "cyfyngedig"
225 cym	Newid dyddiad cyfeirnod cyfrifeg
287 cym	Newid lleoliad neu gyferiad y Swyddfa Gofrestredig
288a cym	PENODI cyfarwyddwr neu ysgrifennydd
288b cym	YMDDEOLIAD cyfarwyddwr neu ysgrifennydd
288c cym	NEWID MANYLION cyfarwyddwr neu ysgrifennydd
363 cym	Ffyrflen Flynyddol

363 cym	Dalen Barhad	
363 cym	Rhestr o aelodau gorffennol a phresennol - Atodiad I ffurflen 363 cym	
652a cym	Cais am ddileu o'r gofrestr	
652a cym	Dalen Barhad	
652c cym	Tynnu'n ol gais am ddileu o'r gofrestr	

Section G: Investment company with variable capital forms

IC 65(2)	Location of Directors' Service Contracts and Register of Members or of any Change in their Location
IC 65(4a)	Notice of Change of Head Office Address
IC 65(4b)	Notice of Change of Director
IC 65(4c)	Notice of Change of Depositary
IC 65(4d)	Notice of Change of Particulars of a Depositary or Director

Section H: Limited Liability partnership forms

LLP2	Application for incorporation of a Limited Liability partnership (and continuation sheet)
LLP3	Notice of change of name of a Limited Liability Partnership
LLP8	Notice of designated members of a Limited Liability Partnership
LLP190	Location of register of debenture holders of a Limited Liability Partnership
LLP225	Change of accounting reference date of a Limited Liability Partnership

LLP244	Notice of extension of accounts delivery period of a Limited Liability Partnership
LLP287	Change in Situation or Address of Registered Office of a Limited Liability Partnership
LLP287a	Notice that the Registered Office Address of a Limited Liability Partnership is Situated in Wales
LLP288a	Appointment of a Member to a Limited Liability Partnership
LLP288b	Terminating the membership of a Member of a Limited Liability Partnership
LLP288c	Change of Particulars of a Member of a Limited Liability Partnership
LLP363	Annual return of a Limited Liability Partnership (and continuation sheet)
LLP391	Notice of removal of auditor from a Limited Liability Partnership
LLP395	Particulars of a charge in respect of a Limited Liability Partnership
LLP397	Particulars for the registration of a charge to secure a series of debentures in respect of a Limited Liability Partnership
LLP397a	Particulars of an issue of secured debentures in a series in respect of a Limited Liability Partnership
LLP398	Limited Liability Partnership: Certificate of registration in Scotland or Northern Ireland of a charge comprising property situated there
LLP400	Particulars of a mortgage or charge on a property that has been acquired by a Limited Liability Partnership
LLP401	Register of charges, memoranda of satisfaction and appointments and cessations of receivers

LLP403a	Limited Liability Partnership: Declaration of satisfaction in full or part of mortgage or charge
LLP403b	Declaration that part of the property or undertaking charged (a) has been released from the charge;(b) no longer forms part of the limited liability partnership's property or undertaking
LLP405(1)	Notice of appointment of receiver or manager in respect of a Limited Liability Partnership
LLP405(2)	Notice of ceasing to act as receiver or manager in respect of a Limited Liability partnership
LLP652a	Application for striking off a Limited Liability Partnership
LLP625c	Withdrawal of Application for voluntary strike off a Limited Liability Partnership

Section I: Other forms available

CH23	Public Search (Complaint as to absence of statutory documents)
DEB 15	Specimen ordinary/special resolution
DEB 8	Dormant company resolution
DEB18	Specimen format for non trading accounts
L1	Should I be registered for VAT?
ML7	Microfiche Complaint ticket
NC 19	Special resolution on change of name
POS2	Postal Search information leaflet, plus order form.
DCA	Dormant Company Accounts pro forma

appendix F

Company statistics

Number of companies on the active register

	England and Wales	Scotland	Great Britain
31st March 1998	1,119,400	65,500	1,184,900
31st March 1999	1,211,800	69,300	1,281,100
31st March 2000	1,288,500	73,100	1,361,600
31st March 2001	1,364,900	77,400	1,442,300
31st March 2002	1,410,700	80,800	1,491,500
28th February 2003	1,529,385	87,995	1,617,380

New company incorporations

	Year to 31-03-00	Year to 31-03-01	Year to 31-03-02
Public (includes conversion from private)	5,800	5,600	5,100
Unlimited private	200	200	300
Private limited by shares (includes conversion from public)	214,200	227,000	214,300
Private limited by guarantee	5,400	5,400	5,800
	225,600	238,200	225,500

Disqualification orders made against directors

Year to 31st March 1998	1,460
Year to 31st March 1999	1,484
Year to 31st March 2000	1,744
Year to 31st March 2001	1,700
Year to 31st March 2002	1,929

Number of Documents filed at Companies House

	Year to 31-03-00	Year to 31-03-01	Year to 31-03-02
New registrations	225,000	236,000	225,000
Annual returns	1,114,000	1,187,000	1,260,000
Annual accounts	999,000	1,061,000	1,144,000
All other	3,209,000	3,454,000	3,433,000
	5,547,000	5,938,000	6,062,000

N.B. Some of the figures in this appendix have been rounded.

index

Index

accounts

abbreviated accounts 43

accounting reference date...39

approval of 44

auditor's report...42

content of..40

dormant companies 47

filing with registrar of companies 45

first accounts...39

medium-sized companies 43

preparing accounts and keeping records.....................................38

publication of...44, 46

signature of...44

small companies...43

administration

concept of...159

conclusion of..162

early stages of 161

effects of 161

later stages of 162

purposes of..160

administration order

grounds for obtaining...160

administrator

appointment of..159

alternate director 18

annual general meeting...112

annual return

example of a completed form 186

in detail..182

shuttle system...179

time limits for filing 178

auditor's report 42

board meetings

articles and Table A 134

calling of...135

chairman...137

committees and other meetings...140

deficiency in the number of directors.....................................138

directors' interests 136

due notice 135

electronic board meetings...141

minutes..138

quorum...136

written resolutions 138

chairman

of board meetings..137

of general meetings 126

Companies House

addresses 246

CD roms 205

Companies House Direct 205

electronic filing 206

forms 197

guidance booklets 247

list of forms 275

monitor..204

obtaining information from...202

penalties and prosecutions...200

quality of documents filed..199

requirements to file resolutions 198

website 204

company seal...34

company secretary

appointment..7

as an officer of the company..8

newly formed company 7

other duties 10

removal...7

responsibilities on appointment of a director............................17

responsibilities on removal of a director...................................17

statutory duties of 8

who may hold the position of?...6

confidentiality orders...33

CREST..145

crown preference 170

debentures

    bearer debenture...81

    debenture stock..81

    definition of...80

    fixed charges 83

    floating charges 83

    power to issue 82

    registered debenture 81

    registration of charges..85

    stamp duty...84

    transferability..84

    trust deed 85

    trustees..84

directors

    age restriction..14

    alternate directors 18

    appointment by existing directors...15

    appoint by members 15

    appointment of the first directors..15

    company stationery (names on)...20

    compensation for loss of office 18

    de facto director..12

    deficiency in the number of directors...138

    death of 16

    disqualification by court order...16

    directors' interests 136

    indemnity 18

    inspection of directors' service contracts 20

    insurance 18

    loans to 20

    number of 20

    receipt by the company of a members' resolution to remove.....18

    removal by the members..16

    removal by the other directors...16

    removal of the first directors...15

    removal on the grounds of bankruptcy..16

    removal on the grounds of age..16

    remuneration...18

    responsibilities of 19

    rights of 17

rotation of 15

shadow directors...13

share qualification 14

undischarged bankrupt 14

what makes a person a director?.................................12

dividends

dividend warrants..55

funds available for payment of 52

procedure for declaration of 53

procedure for payment of 53

scrip dividends 56

significance of different classes of share 53

tax vouchers...55

elective regime...117

extraordinary general meeting................................114

fees permitted for inspection of registers................27

general meetings

annual general meeting 112

chairman...126

convening of..120

details and contents of notice 123

elective regime 117

electronic general meetings 129

entitlement to receive notice 121

extraordinary general meeting 114

minutes...128

notice of resolutions..114

notice sent by means of electronic communication ...123

period of notice..121

proxies 124

quorum..125

resolutions..114

requisitioning of 120

voting 14

instalments on shares 64

interest

funds available for payment of 52

licensed insolvency practitioners 172

loan stock 82

medium-sized companies

    accounts of 43

meetings

    see under board meetings and general meetings

memorandum of association

    authorised share capital 96

    limited liability 96

    name of the company 90

    objects of the company 94

    public company 96

    registered office 93

    subscription clause 96

minors as shareholders 66

minutes

    of a board meeting 138

    of a general meeting 128

name of the company 90

notice

    of board meetings 135

    of general meetings 121

    of resolutions at general meetings 114

    sent by means of electronic communication 123

objects of the company 94

pre-emption rights on the issue of shares 74

proxies 124

quorum

    at board meetings 136

    at general meetings 125

receivership 157

resolutions

elective resolution 115

extraordinary resolution 114

ordinary resolution 116

special notice of an ordinary resolution 116

special resolution 115

written resolution of directors 138

written resolution of members 117

seal 34

serious loss of capital by a public company 65

shares

acquisition by a company of its own 76

bearer shares 146

CREST 145

financial assistance and the acquisition of 75

forged transfers 146

issue at a discount 73

issue at a premium 73

issue of, for cash 70

issue of, for non-cash consideration 72

pre-emption rights 74

share certificates 149

stamp duty 150

transfer of 144

transmission of 147

shareholders

minors 66

nominee shareholders 65

share capital

authorised 60, 96

calls on 64

carrying multiple votes 64

instalments on 64

issued 61

non-voting shares 63

ordinary shares 63

preference shares 62

reduction of 75

serious loss of capital by a public company 65

single-member companies...119

small company

    accounts of...43

stamp duty...84, 150

stationery

    disclosure of information 97

statutory registers

    copies of...25

    fees permitted for inspection and copies...................27

    inspection of 25

    location of 25

stock transfer form

    example of..152

striking-off

    at the instigation of the registrar.............................174

    following an application by the company.................173

Table A

    comment on 105

    complete reproduction of...209

    relating to board meetings 134

Table C

    comment on 108

    complete reproduction of...241

tax vouchers 55

unsecured loan stock 82

winding up of companies

    creditors' voluntary winding up...............................168

    crown preference – abolition of 170

    licensed insolvency practitioners.............................172

    members' voluntary winding up 167

    order of priority in the distribution of funds 171

    winding up by the court 169

Thorogood publishing

Thorogood publishes a wide range of books, reports, special briefings, psychometric tests and videos. Listed below is a selection of key titles.

Desktop Guides

The marketing strategy desktop guide	*Norton Paley* • £16.99
The sales manager's desktop guide	*Mike Gale and Julian Clay* • £16.99
The company director's desktop guide	*David Martin* • £16.99
The credit controller's desktop guide	*Roger Mason* • £16.99
The company secretary's desktop guide	*Roger Mason* • £16.99
The finance and accountancy desktop guide	*Ralph Tiffin* • £16.99
The commercial engineer's desktop guide	*Tim Boyce* • £16.99
The training manager's desktop guide	*Eddie Davies* • £16.99
The PR practitioner's desktop guide	*Caroline Black* • £16.99
Win new business – the desktop guide	*Susan Croft* • £16.99

Masters in Management

Mastering business planning and strategy	*Paul Elkin* • £14.99
Mastering financial management	*Stephen Brookson* • £14.99
Mastering leadership	*Michael Williams* • £14.99
Mastering marketing	*Ian Ruskin-Brown* • £16.99
Mastering negotiations	*Eric Evans* • £14.99
Mastering people management	*Mark Thomas* • £14.99
Mastering personal and interpersonal skills	*Peter Haddon* • £14.99
Mastering project management	*Cathy Lake* • £14.99

Business Action Pocketbooks

Edited by David Irwin

Building your business pocketbook	£6.99
Developing yourself and your staff pocketbook	£6.99
Finance and profitability pocketbook	£6.99
Managing and employing people pocketbook	£6.99
Sales and marketing pocketbook	£6.99
Managing projects and operations pocketbook	£6.99
Effective business communications pocketbook	£6.99
PR techniques that work	*Edited by Jim Dunn* • £6.99
Adair on leadership	*Edited by Neil Thomas* • £6.99

Other titles

The complete guide to international accounting standards	*Ralph Tiffin and David Young* • £18.99
The complete guide to debt recovery	*Roger Mason* • £12.99
The John Adair handbook of management and leadership	*Edited by Neil Thomas* • £12.99
The inside track to successful management	*Dr Gerald Kushel* • £12.99
The pension trustee's handbook (3rd edition)	*Robin Ellison* • £25
Boost your company's profits	*Barrie Pearson* • £12.99
Negotiate to succeed	*Julie Lewthwaite* • £12.99
The management tool kit	*Sultan Kermally* • £10.99
Working smarter	*Graham Roberts-Phelps* • £14.99
Test your management skills	*Michael Williams* • £15.99
The art of headless chicken management	*Elly Brewer and Mark Edwards* • £6.99
Everything you need for an NVQ in management	*Julie Lewthwaite* • £22.99
Customer relationship management	*Graham Roberts-Phelps* • £14.99
Sales management and organisation	*Peter Green* • £10.99
Telephone tactics	*Graham Roberts-Phelps* • £10.99
Companies don't succeed people do!	*Graham Roberts-Phelps* • £12.99
Inspiring leadership	*John Adair* • £15.99
The book of ME	*Barrie Pearson and Neil Thomas* • £14.99
Dynamic practice development	*Kim Tasso* • £19.99

Gurus on business strategy	*Tony Grundy* • £14.99
The concise Adair on leadership	*Edited by Neil Thomas* • £9.99
The concise time management and personal development	
	Adair and Melanie Allen • £9.99
Successful selling solutions	*Julian Clay* • £12.99
Gurus on marketing	*Sultan Kermally* • £14.99
The concise Adair on communication and presentation skills	
	Edited by Neil Thomas • £9.99
High performance consulting skills	*Mark Thomas* • £15.99
Developing and managing talent	*Sultan Kermally* • £14.99

Thorogood also has an extensive range of reports and special briefings which are written specifically for professionals wanting expert information.

For a full listing of all Thorogood publications, or to order any title, please call Thorogood Customer Services on 020 7749 4748 or fax on 020 7729 6110. Alternatively view our website at **www.thorogood.ws**.

Focused on developing your potential

Falconbury, the sister company to Thorogood publishing, brings together the leading experts from all areas of management and strategic development to provide you with a comprehensive portfolio of action-centred training and learning.

We understand everything managers and leaders need to **be, know and do** to succeed in today's commercial environment. Each product addresses a different technical or personal development need that will encourage growth and increase your potential for success.

- Practical public training programmes
- Tailored in-company training
- Coaching
- Mentoring
- Topical business seminars
- Trainer bureau/bank
- Adair Leadership Foundation

The most valuable resource in any organisation is its people; it is essential that you invest in the development of your management and leadership skills to ensure your team fulfil their potential. Investment into both personal and professional development has been proven to provide an outstanding ROI through increased productivity in both you and your team. Ultimately leading to a dramatic impact on the bottom line.

With this in mind Falconbury have developed a comprehensive portfolio of training programmes to enable managers of all levels to develop their skills in leadership, communications, finance, people management, change management and all areas vital to achieving success in today's commercial environment.

What Falconbury can offer you?
- Practical applied methodology with a proven results
- Extensive bank of experienced trainers
- Limited attendees to ensure one-to-one guidance
- Up to the minute thinking on management and leadership techniques
- Interactive training
- Balanced mix of theoretical and practical learning
- Learner-centred training
- Excellent cost/quality ratio

Falconbury In-Company Training

Falconbury are aware that a public programme may not be the solution to leadership and management issues arising in your firm. Involving only attendees from your organisation and tailoring the programme to focus on the current challenges you face individually and as a business may be more appropriate. With this in mind we have brought together our most motivated and forward thinking trainers to deliver tailored in-company programmes developed specifically around the needs within your organisation.

All our trainers have a practical commercial background and highly refined people skills. During the course of the programme they act as facilitator, trainer and mentor, adapting their style to ensure that each individual benefits equally from their knowledge to develop new skills.

Falconbury works with each organisation to develop a programme of training that fits your needs.

Mentoring and coaching

Developing and achieving your personal objectives in the workplace is becoming increasingly difficult in today's constantly changing environment. Additionally, as a manager or leader, you are responsible for guiding colleagues towards the realisation of their goals. Sometimes it is easy to lose focus on your short and long-term aims.

Falconbury's one-to-one coaching draws out individual potential by raising self-awareness and understanding, facilitating the learning and performance development that creates excellent managers and leaders. It builds renewed self-confidence and a strong sense of 'can-do' competence, contributing significant benefit to the organisation. Enabling you to focus your energy on developing your potential and that of your colleagues.

Mentoring involves formulating winning strategies, setting goals, monitoring achievements and motivating the whole team whilst achieving a much improved work life balance.

Falconbury – Business Legal Seminars

Falconbury Business Legal Seminars specialises in the provision of high quality training for legal professionals from both in-house and private practice internationally.

The focus of these events is to provide comprehensive and practical training on current international legal thinking and practice in a clear and informative format.

Event subjects include, drafting commercial agreements, employment law, competition law, intellectual property, managing an in-house legal department and international acquisitions.

For more information on all our services please contact Falconbury on +44 (0) 20 7729 6677 or visit the website at: www.falconbury.co.uk.